Managing Marketing Profitability

Managing
Marketing Profitability

Sanford R. Simon

American Management Association, Inc.

Standard book number: 8144–2123–7
Library of Congress catalog card number: 79–82261

Acknowledgments

THE partners, managers, senior consultants, and associates at Touche, Ross, Bailey & Smart will find many of their experiences, thoughts, and cases within the covers of this book. In any cooperative endeavor there are always a few who must be singled out for special contribution. We particularly want to thank Dr. Victor H. Brown, Max F. Sporer, Richard D. Major, and David V. Burchfield, who participated in the original Managing Marketing Profitability Seminars and who put together many of the original examples in this book. Also, Robert L. Burton, who constantly read, challenged, and edited our work, and Charles Stamm, Joseph Di Mario, and Laurence Garter, who assisted with several chapters. Lastly, I want to thank my wife, whose patience during the many hours of writing was so necessary.

SANFORD R. SIMON

Foreword

THE THEME of this book is profitable marketing. Its
purpose is to offer executives an alternative discipline to the purely
behavioral-oriented or sales approaches to defining the marketer's
role in business.

Its origin stems from management services practice at Touche,
Ross, Bailey & Smart, where the primary discipline is a managerial and quantitative approach to business. This discipline
is detailed by Robert Beyer, Managing Partner of the firm, in the
book *Profitability Accounting for Planning and Control*. In this book,
however, we will present some of these philosophies as they may be
adapted by a marketing executive.

We wish to make executives more aware of the planning and
control tools available to marketers. Thus we will define applicable
profit concepts and illustrate their use in a series of case studies.

All too often, marketing personnel have been victims of cred-
ibility gaps created by men who have sold management on the
smell, feel, and emotion of merchandising. Often this emotion has
had little relationship to the world of profits and return on dollars
invested. To change this image, we have developed a functional,
profit-oriented approach to marketing, and hope that you will
find this book a readable, enjoyable guide.

Contents

Chapter I

The Measurement of Profit

I<small>F</small> <small>FOUR MEN</small> sat in a room, one an advertising man, another a salesman, the third a physical distribution specialist, and the fourth a market researcher, each one might be a "marketer" by present definition. The reason for the vast range in defining the term is that marketing has not matured as a profession. Marketing is a vast area of commercial activity that exists from the point in the manufacturing cycle where the production line ends to the point of final sale and delivery.

Marketing and, indeed, all of business, exist to make a profit. The common factor in advertising, distribution, sales, and market research is identifying the opportunities that one expects to result in profitable sales. Marketing requires that money and energy be expended to create the sale. In a basic marketing text, such as Maynard and Beckman's *Principles of Marketing*, the magnitude and complexity of the marketing task, the number of persons employed and the income they derive from the marketing activity, and the number of marketing institutions, as well as the cost of marketing, are listed as reasons which make marketing important.

The heart of marketing, however, lies in its sales and promotional aspects—finding customers and inducing them to buy. In this sense, marketing is the dynamic force in business by which production is generated and related to a steady seeking out of the markets for goods.

The cost of this task has been identified in various forms. Marketing costs are said to range from 28 percent to 33 percent of the Gross National Product, and a Twentieth Century Fund study concluded that marketing costs equaled 59 cents of the consumer's dollar. Regardless of how many gross dollars are expended in marketing, most companies find the marketing dollar a significant part of the cost of doing business. For example, in a cosmetics or a toy company, it is not unusual that 35 cents to 37 cents of a dollar are spent in manufacture. The remaining 63 cents to 65 cents represent the cost of the marketing effort and the amount reserved for a planned profit. A marketer must understand basic terms of accounting.

CURRENT ACCOUNTING SYSTEMS

There are currently three major types of accounting: custodial accounting, performance accounting, and decision-oriented accounting.

Custodial accounting. This is financial accounting for the enterprise. Its output is the reports and data from which management reports the condition of the business primarily to external interests such as stockholders, government, and securities exchanges.

Performance accounting. This is the matching of performance statistics against plans. It includes accounting procedures and reports which exist to facilitate performance evaluation. It also includes the functions of responsibility accounting, that is, the collection of costs by centers of responsibility within the organization, and utilizes financial data other than costs. This may include product line revenue, physical workload statistics, and internal reports. Standards and budgets are used and developed as control is required. In addition, performance accounting measures actual performance against planned performance by responsibility.

Decision-oriented accounting. This is the use of accounting and statistical information for the evaluation of alternative courses of action. It includes the financial and statistical techniques providing quantitative information in the form which can best assist in making management decisions. This includes information for profit planning, such as product pricing, make or buy, inventory policies, and choice of alternative production methods. In this area, business has traditionally depended on special analyses and memorandum accounts.

In this book we seek to integrate the concepts of performance and decision-oriented accounting, which are often referred to as techniques of managerial accounting. The specific information applicable to the marketing function, whether it be advertising, sales, physical distribution, or internal cost structures, provides the body of knowledge necessary for true marketing control.

The Growing Importance of Marketing Costs

In the dynamics of today's business world a manager must control marketing costs to survive. The cost of the marketing effort, including sales and sales promotion or advertising, often exceeds the company's profit.

In controlling marketing costs, the business manager must rely upon his company's accounting system. The accounting system is the language of business, cutting across all areas of production, purchasing, and marketing. Supplemented by statistical analysis, it forms the basis for decisions to be quantified by the marketer.

Typically, most accounting systems are designed to perform a custodial or caretaking function and are not necessarily designed to respond to the marketer's or manager's need for decision-making information. They tell a manager what has happened in great detail, but do not show how costs will react in the future. For the decision maker, the future performance of his costs is more important than history. Accountants in education, industry, and the professions often have not provided business managers with information needed to run their enterprises. They have tried to teach managers accounting, instead of tailoring accounting to meet business needs. The result has been a wide gap between the "providers" of information, the accountants, and the "users" of information, the marketer or business manager. This gap did not always exist.

A HISTORICAL VIEW OF ACCOUNTING

The earliest business systems responded directly to the needs of merchants. They were designed by merchants and were used to account for the transactions of their businesses. The medieval Venetian trader had little difficulty logging each venture. Until the Middle Ages, the only persons other than the merchants using their logs or ledgers concerned with accounting functions were government and Church bodies (primarily for tax purposes). History reveals that Charlemagne required annual inventories, and Henry I of England required annual audits.

The Italian or Venetian system of double-entry bookkeeping was formalized by an Italian monk, Luca Pacioli, in 1494 in a book entitled *Summa Arithmetica, Geometria, Proporcionita*. This system spread throughout Europe by the end of the Middle Ages. It is interesting that a Scotsman, George A. Wattsman of Edinburgh, is said to have been the first full-time practicing accountant, in the late 1600's. Some marketers or merchants would claim that this was the beginning of their problems.

It was the dual growth of governmental needs for tax revenues and stock exchange requirements for reporting that channeled the development of traditional or custodial systems of accounting. The need for annual or periodic custodial reports causes the separation of managerial operating statistics from custodial information within the business. In West Virginia Pulp & Paper Company's booklet *A History of the Annual Report*, the growth frequency and content of annual reports is traced. In the United States there were relatively few annual reports during the 19th century. Most businesses were single proprietorships or partnerships, and it was believed that no outsider had need to know how they were doing. This changed as the increasing momentum of the Industrial Revolution created the need for risk capital, and statements had to be presented for those who provided capital, the stockholders. Governments became concerned with the content and quality of reports, both to form a basis for taxation and to protect investors.

Before 1900, only 16 of our states required corporate reports, including details of assets and liabilities. Five states required just a general, often verbal, statement of a corporation's condition. By 1895 the New York Stock Exchange recommended that annual reports be published at least 15 days prior to annual meetings. In 1899 this became part of the listing requirement. Companies had to publish at least once a year a "properly detailed statement of income and expenditures for such preceding period, and also a balance sheet, giving a detailed and accurate statement of the corporation or the company at the close of its last fiscal year of recent date."

These requirements of public listing and those imposed by the Internal Revenue Service forced the constraints that form the modern corporate "custodial" accounting system, and by the early 1900's the concepts we live with today were well-accepted principles. These custodial accounting concepts are:

- The period cost. This is the practice of assigning costs to time periods in which they are incurred or to which they have accrued.
- Full absorption costing. This is the practice of assigning all direct and indirect manufacturing costs to products and carrying the costs through inventory into cost of sales.

The period cost concept matches revenues with the costs necessary to produce the revenues. The matching of revenues (benefits) and costs (efforts and materials) in the form of accruals or deferrals will often cause the accounting for programs which occur in multiple time periods to become of secondary concern to the accountant. Both of these notions help insure consistency of accounting treatment among businesses and make periodic income statements meaningful; both make management reporting more difficult, however. Managers seeking basic cost information receive "full absorption cost" as a "true cost." Full absorption costs generally cannot be considered meaningful "true costs" for management use. Costs are decision-making tools. The fully absorbed cost gives a blurred and often distorted picture. The appropriateness of the fully absorbed cost depends upon the decision, the basis for absorption, the number of products produced, and the type of business being measured.

The balance sheet portrays the financial position of the business

at the end of an accounting period. The operating statement or
P&L statement reflects the results of operations for a specific period
of time. Costs are "matched" against the revenue; unsold units
of production are "inventoried" at the full absorption cost.

The financial statements derived from a custodial accounting
system portray the business to the outside world. They do not
reflect the opportunistic realities of the "venture" or which of a
manager's various products are profitable. In order to be profit-
oriented, a manager requires reports that portray the business as
it exists, and portray performance. A good managerial accounting
system will supply this added dimension.

THE APPLICATION OF MANAGERIAL ACCOUNTING

In order to understand the profit impact of a decision, a marketing executive needs accounting and marketing information
displayed in a manner that is responsive to his methods of decision
making. His marketing information system must portray the effect
on profit of market performance variations from plan, which
can be analyzed in terms of volume, price, mix, and budgeted
cost. The volume, price, and mix variances are deviations from the
planned standard profit contribution that should be realized from
sales. The budgeted cost variance is most commonly used and
shows the fluctuations in profit caused by changes in expenses.
The separate effects on profit because of deviation of planned sales
volumes, planned sales mix, or a variation in pricing of products can be isolated only when a standard profit contribution by
a unit of product and by the total product line is established.

If these performance measures are used in their most effective
manner, they must be made applicable to the marketing areas
measured, such as the salesman working in his territory. If data
are properly defined and then collected, the information applicable to one salesman in a territory, selling a specific product to
a unique type of account, can be determined. The building block
structure of cost and revenue data must be defined, nevertheless,
so that information can be meaningful when collected into product
line or responsibility centers. In other words, the profit concepts
applicable to marketers using standard direct cost systems should

permit the employment of data building blocks which allow the evaluation of products and responsibility within the company.

The information system must be capable of sorting the data building blocks into meaningful "user oriented" reports. The executive should be able to select his object of measurement, be it a sales territory, product, channel of distribution, or account, and receive valid revenue and cost information applicable to that object. Only by receiving valid information can good decisions be made.

Our objective in this book is to define the information requirements of a profit-oriented marketing information system. We will utilize these concepts to show how a reporting system can be designed to provide for the tracking of exceptions to plans through an organization from corporate operations reports to increasingly detailed reports, showing results by areas of responsibility. A good reporting system provides each responsible person with the information he requires, at the time needed, and in the most useful form. Utilizing this concept, a manager will receive quantitative information to evaluate performance and then be assured that the "scorekeeping" will portray meaningful results.

Chapter II

Marketing Costs

A VENETIAN TRADER had no problem defining his marketing cost structure. Indeed, he had no dilemma with his elementary bookkeeping system, or in defining terms, such as a modern executive has. These problems of definition, which will be detailed in the following chapter, can cause anxiety when a businessman tries to isolate the costs that affect his particular area of responsibility. The Venetian trader loaded merchandise on a ship, sent the ship to sea, and when his venture was complete, the shipowner knew his profit at once. If the ship did not return he could ascertain the extent of his loss.

Things are not that simple today. Under modern custodial accounting, we are forced away from accounting on a venture basis and into a structure tied to "period" costs and allocations that distort the view of the venture. The conventional accounting system portrays the condition of the business, not its function or "doing." Programs, ventures, and responsibilities are subordinated to determining the operating results of the business for a period of time.

It is the manager's job to run functions, programs, and ventures, and to be responsible for their success. This does not necessarily coincide with the mission of the accounting system. One works for success; the other portrays financial condition for the "period ended" to the outside world.

The structure of the present conventional accounting system can be traced to the later years of the Industrial Revolution; by the late 1800's the "inventorying of costs" and "matching" concepts were fairly well fixed and known. In 1913, with the passage of the Internal Revenue Act, the structure implementing these concepts became accepted.

The concept of inventorying costs grew with increased industrialization. For accounting purposes those costs were matched against revenues. Because of their tangible nature, manufacturing costs such as those for labor and material were matchable, and accountants were able to show them "in inventory" at the ends of production cycles and reporting periods. Other costs, such as those for sales, administration, and general purposes, were nonindustrial as well as nonmatchable, and the practice grew to charge these costs in the applicable accounting period. However, selling and promotion costs were charged in periods that did not coincide with the period when the benefit of the expenditure was to be realized. The result of employing the concepts of matching costs and period costs can be seen in the conventional gross profit-net profit, profit-and-loss statement:

Conceptual Profit-and-Loss Statement

	Sales	(Current revenue)
Less:	Cost of goods sold	(Matchable mfg. cost)
	Gross profit	
Less:		
	Selling expense	(Periodic or non-
	General and administrative expense	matchable costs)
	Profit before taxes	

The problem of the marketer is that marketing decisions do not neatly fit this traditional concept of matching of funds. Much of marketing deals with ventures. The matching of costs and revenues must show how the ventures or programs of a business are performing. Many costs of ventures involve programs such as special campaigns, introductory offers, research, and new product development. These costs must be assigned in a way that allows the portrayal of the individual program's profitability. In other words, money spent on a program today, in one time period, may not show a revenue stream, or profit, until a future period. Management has the right and the need to plan and control these streams of cost, revenue, and profit.

This is not a requirement of the custodial accounting system, which portrays the condition of an entire business; the users of information in a company, the managers and decision makers, need information in formats and components that are not the same as the custodial structure.

The information provider, the controller's department, must see that the requirements of the user are served. The corporate executive, production manager, and marketer are users of information. If necessary, the information should be tailored to their individual decision-making needs.

In a simplified form one of the traps inherent in the matching concept can be shown. In this example, Exhibit 1, it appears that the more that is produced, the more profit will be made. There is no relationship to the reality of the market—that is, in each case the same quantity was sold.

Gross profit is revenue minus cost of sales. If the gross profit concept and the logic of Exhibit 1 are followed, the way to make the product line more profitable per unit is to produce more. This would seem to be fallacious; the true relationship of the contribution per unit sold toward the fixed cost and profit is not clear. The contribution of the unit when sold is shown in Exhibit 2.

We have depicted the marginal income concept in its simplest form. On an applicable unit, product line, or functional basis the accounting system in use for the decision process must show how costs will behave during the decision cycle. Looking at Exhibit 2, the marketer knows he has a $12.00 contribution from each sale and $12.00 of marginal income to apply to fixed costs and to provide for a profit.

Situation:	Make 2 units Sell 1 unit	Make 3 units Sell 1 unit
	Production Costs	*Production Costs*
Materials	$ 2	$ 3
Labor	2	3
Power	2	3
Rent	10	10
Total cost	$16	$19
Cost per unit	$ 8	$ 6.33
	Sales Cost Match	*Sales Cost Match*
Revenue	$15.00	$15.00
Cost	8.00	6.33
Indicated profit	$ 7.00	$ 8.67

Exhibit 1

CONTRIBUTION ANALYSIS

Unit sales price	$15.00
Direct costs	3.00
Unit contribution	$12.00
Units sold	2
Total contribution toward fixed costs and profit	$24.00
Fixed cost of rent	10.00
Indicated profit	$14.00

Exhibit 2

Marketing Costs Defined

Marketing costs are the costs of getting and filling orders, the two major functions of marketing. By dividing the cost structure into these categories, financial data can be sorted to the marketing cost functions of advertising, sales, sales discounts or sales deductions, freight, and distribution.

The order-getting vs. order-filling data "sort" or "cut," together with their associated functions, are shown in Exhibit 3. This sort forms the basis for the managerial cost analyst's reports.

Elements of Marketing Costs

The elements of marketing costs in a managerial accounting system fall into six categories. The first three, which are planned, direct, incremental costs, are as follows:

1. Specific sales deductions. These are deductions such as cash discounts, trade discounts, and freight out. These are noninventoriable costs specifically incurred because of a sale. They are variable in that they are incurred at a rate directly relatable to the number of sales made.
2. Specification costs. These are costs for direct material and direct labor involved in the manufacture of a production unit. These are inventoriable costs which are specifically identified with a unit of product in standard amounts, which can be obtained from bills of material and operation sheets.
3. Variable overhead. This includes all normal recurring costs which are not specifically identifiable with an individual production unit but which vary directly with volume in some manner.

These three categories of planned direct incremental costs form the first part of the contribution format as shown in Exhibit 2. By subtracting these on a per unit basis from a unit selling price, the unit's profit contribution to nonincremental costs can be obtained. The next two categories include all planned costs which are

CONCEPTUAL FRAMEWORK FOR MARKETING COST ANALYSIS

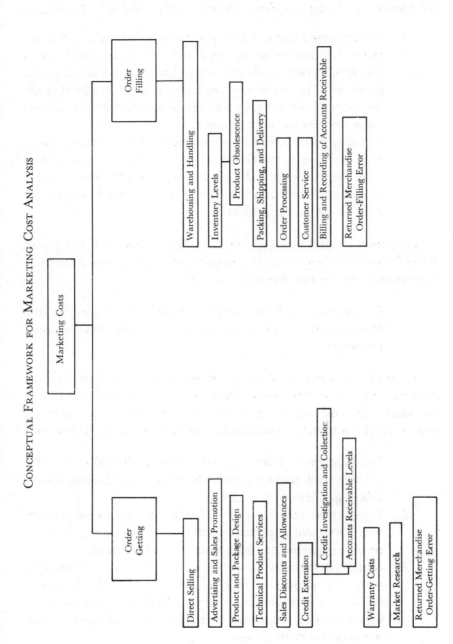

Marketing Costs

Order Getting
- Direct Selling
- Advertising and Sales Promotion
- Product and Package Design
- Technical Product Services
- Sales Discounts and Allowances
- Credit Extension
  - Credit Investigation and Collection
  - Accounts Receivable Levels
- Warranty Costs
- Market Research
- Returned Merchandise Order-Getting Error

Order Filling
- Warehousing and Handling
- Inventory Levels
  - Product Obsolescence
- Packing, Shipping, and Delivery
- Order Processing
- Customer Service
- Billing and Recording of Accounts Receivable
- Returned Merchandise Order-Filling Error

Exhibit 3

not incremental (do not vary directly with volume). They are:

4. Programmed costs. These are the costs for which a com-
    pany is committed in relatively fixed amounts for a
    specified period, such as a year. They are incurred as the
    result of a management decision, and generally include
    the costs of advertising, market or product research, and
    some nonroutine maintenance.

5. Standby costs. These are costs such as depreciation, prop-
    erty taxes, and salaries of key personnel, which include
    all costs which would be incurred, even at zero volume,
    in order to maintain the company in a position of readi-
    ness to serve or produce.

Programmed and standby costs are, in reality, two categories
of fixed costs. The last of the six categories includes all the deviations
from plan from the first five elements of costs:

6. Cost variances. These include all deviations from standard
    budgeted or programmed costs and from planned sales
    discounts.

In understanding how such elements affect a project, the
marketer must see how these costs behave or react when sales
are made. In cost behavior there are only two basic patterns,
and a third pattern, a combination of the first two. These are:

1. Variable cost. This is a cost that varies directly with
    volume and includes such items as commissions, direct
    labor, and direct material.

2. Fixed (nonvariable) cost. This is an expense that does
    not vary with volume of activity; for example, most
    rents, management costs, and some sales salaries.

3. Managed (decision) cost. This is a cost set by manage-
    ment for planning periods and varies with increased
    activity at management decision. Such costs are involved
    in advertising appropriations, incentive payments, and
    for periodic clerical help.

These three cost patterns are charted in Exhibit 4.

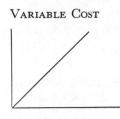

VARIABLE COST

Expense

Volume

FIXED COST

Expense

Volume

MANAGED COST

Expense

Volume

Exhibit 4

The six cost elements and the three patterns of cost behavior can be portrayed in an operations statement, based upon marginal cost concepts. This is shown in Exhibit 5.

PROFIT CONTRIBUTION ANALYSIS—PRODUCT LINE
XYZ COMPANY

Sales (10,000 units at $1.00 each)			$10,000
Less: Direct variable costs			
Direct labor	$1,500		
Direct materials	1,200		
Variable overhead	1,000	3,700	
Profit contribution		6,300	
Less: Specific product-line expenses (nonvariable-programmed)			
Advertising	$1,000		
Promotion	500		
Market research	500	2,000	
Less: Standby (specific fixed)			
Depreciation	500		
Product-line management	500	1,000	3,000
Product-line contribution*			$ 3,300

*This is the contribution to cover the general corporate overhead and profits that have not been allocated to the product lines.

Exhibit 5

In this exhibit the variable costs of direct labor, direct materials, and variable overhead have been segregated and subtracted from sales. By so doing we can compute the profit contribution to be received from each additional unit of product sold. The marketer now knows that, from the sale of an additional product unit, he will receive an additional 63 cents as profit contribution.

The fixed, decision, and standby costs of the product line have also been segregated in this statement. This allows us to see which costs are variable and which costs are fixed and how they may respond to the decision process. These programmed and standby costs will exist as long as we have the product line. After they are covered we can see if there is a contribution from this product line to the corporate overhead and profit. In effect, a profit contribution remains after the variable costs are deducted from the sales dollar. A product-line contribution results when the nonvariable direct-product costs are deducted. This product-line contribution represents a contribution to the nonproduct assignable corporate cost structure and toward profits. By analyzing costs in this format, the marketer can determine the contribution of each product within his product line to corporate overhead and profit.

If we accept the concept that it is good to know how much each product in a product line contributes to corporate overhead, we must then answer the following question: "How do you know if you have enough total contribution to provide for the corporation?"

In nonmanagerial-oriented systems each product is allocated a share of corporate overhead. This allocation violates managerial control concepts from a marketing point of view in several ways:

- It buries the true profit contribution of products.
- The allocation is by definition arbitrary.
- The allocation or rate of allocation assumes a production rate that sales personnel can't control.
- An absorbed overhead in a product cost isn't factually valid except where all conditions of its allocation are sufficiently met.

Sufficient profit contribution results from adequate planning, not from overhead absorption. We must plan so that there is sufficient profit generated from the product mix to cover sufficiently the corporate overhead and provide for the desired corporate profit.

PLANNING AND CONTROLLING MARKETING COSTS

To enhance the concepts of marginal contribution, the marketer must utilize profit planning, an evolutionary process which involves the following:

- The setting of overall planning policy.
- The establishment of detailed plans (to the level of product and function).
- The summarization of these plans into a formal profit plan that details financial effects.
- If the initial planned profit proves unsatisfactory, there must be revision of these steps to obtain a final plan that is attainable and satisfactory.

To be successful, this planning process requires management participation at each stage. If they are made responsible for the plan, lower and middle levels of management must assist in formulating it. Top management must establish the initial plan guidelines to direct the planning effort of subordinates, and must spend sufficient time reviewing preliminary plans so that realistic revisions can be suggested. The profit plan which eventually emerges should not be used as a rigid, unalterable yardstick but as a plotted course for management to direct. Deviations from planned performance must result in the firms changing course during the planning year or revising profit goals.

In utilizing the cost analysis concept, a company must plan and control. By reporting against the plan, using it as a basis for comparison, and reacting to variances, a control process is established. In planning and controlling marketing costs the utilization of incremental cost concept is valuable. When paired with a concept of standard costs, the planning and control process allows management additional benefits. Standards are necessarily a planning tool, since they must be conceived in advance of an action. Management can isolate performance variances and changes within a plan and within functions based on standards. Standards are often used in manufacturing but seldom in marketing; they are, however, just as applicable in this latter function.

Standards should be established so that the marketer is responsible only for those marketing costs which occur after goods are transferred to him at standard cost. He should not be responsible for plant, manufacturing, raw material, and other costs beyond his control. The performance of the marketer can thus be measured against price, volume, mix, and budgetary variances.

STANDARD MARKETING COSTS

MARKETING RESPONSIBILITY:

Volume
Price   } Selling variances
Mix

Programmed } Budget variances
Standby

Direct Standard Cost (Transfer Price)

MANUFACTURING RESPONSIBILITY:

Labor
Materials   } Cost variances
Plant overhead
Purchase price

GENERAL OFFICE AND CORPORATE ADMINISTRATION RESPONSIBILITY:

Variances in general, fixed, and corporate budgets

Exhibit 6

The marketer can control his segment of operations only by isolating, through the standard cost mechanism, the marketing cost variances he can influence.

In many companies marketers have been frustrated because price increases triggered by labor or materials cost increases have been transferred to the marketing cost structure in the middle of a planning year. Many of these increases were valid increments that had to be passed on to customers for a firm's operations to remain profitable. However, because of the "scorekeeping" system, these increases were a source of constant abrasion between marketing and other segments of management. The marketer claimed they were affecting his efforts, but could not determine the extent, while management had no means of providing an alternative. The accounting system was not structured to show a price variance, and the overall effect was to blur marketing performance. Had costs and prices been held at standard, and the price increase shown as a reason for variances, the fear or frustration of the marketer would have been reduced.

Exhibit 7

Representative List of Distribution Costs by Function

Direct selling
Salaries
  Administrative and supervisory
  Clerical
  Salesmen
Commissions
Travel and entertainment
Training
Insurance
  Real and personal property
  Liability
  Workmen's compensation
Taxes
  Personal property
  Social Security
  Unemployment insurance
Returned goods expense charge-
  able to salesmen
Pensions
Rent
Utilities
Repairs and maintenance
Depreciation
Postage and office supplies

Advertising and sales promotion
Salaries
  Administrative and supervisory
  Clerical
  Advertising production
Publication space
  Consumer magazines
  Trade journals
  Newspapers
Product promotions
Television time
Advertising supplies
Advertising agency fees
Direct mail expenses
Contest
Conventions and shows
Catalogs and price lists
Cooperative advertising
  Dealers

Retail stores
Billboards

Product and package design
Salaries—administrative and su-
  pervisory
Wages—packaging machine op-
  erators
Materials
Depreciation—packaging machine

Technical product services
Salaries
  Technical representatives
  Clerical
  Administrative
Travel and entertainment
Research and engineering re-
  quests
Laboratory materials
Factory pilot and experimental
  costs

Sales discounts and allowances
Cash discount on sales
Quantity discounts
Sales allowances

Credit extension
Salaries
  Administrative and supervisory
  Credit representatives
  Clerical
Bad debt losses
Forms and postage
Credit rating services
Legal fees—collection efforts
Travel
Financial cost of carrying ac-
  counts receivable

Warranty costs
Advertising material—warranty
  provisions
Warranty claims
  Materials
  Labor

Salaries
  Administrative
  Clerical

Market research
Salaries
  Administrative
  Clerical
Surveys
  Distributors
  Consumers
Industry trade data
Travel

Warehousing and handling
Salaries—administrative
Wages—warehousemen
Depreciation
  Furniture and fixtures
  Power equipment
Insurance
Taxes
Repairs and maintenance
Unsalable merchandise—
    warehouse responsibility
Supplies
Utilities

Inventory levels
Obsolescence markdowns
Financial cost of carrying in-
    ventories

Packing, shipping, and delivery
Salaries
  Administrative
  Clerical
Wages
  Truck drivers
  Truck maintenance men
  Packers
Shipping clerks
Truck operations
Truck repairs
Depreciation
  Furniture and fixtures
  Trucks
Insurance
Taxes

Utilities
Packing supplies
Postage and forms
Freight
  Factory to warehouse
  Warehouse to customer
  Factory to customer
  Outside trucking service

Order processing
Order forms
Salaries—administrative
Wages
  Order review clerks
  Order-processing equipment
    operators
Depreciation—order-processing
    equipment

Customer service
Salaries
  Administrative
  Customer service representa-
    tives
  Clerical
Stationery and supplies

Billing and recording of accounts
  receivable
Sales invoice forms
Salaries
  Clerical
  Administrative
  Accounts receivable clerks
  Sales-invoicing equipment op-
    erators
Depreciation—sales-invoicing
    equipment

Returned merchandise
Freight
Salaries
  Administrative
  Clerical
  Returned goods clerk
Returned goods processing
  Materials
  Labor
  Forms and supplies

Standards allow us to develop the more sophisticated reporting devices employing variances and exception reporting. Later in this book the devices of control, reports, and reporting techniques will be covered in detail.

IDENTIFYING MARKETING COSTS

Most companies do not have a sufficiently detailed chart of accounts to identify marketing costs effectively. These components of a typical marketing cost structure are shown in Exhibit 7, taken from a lighting fixture manufacturer's comprehensive chart of accounts. This chart has been revised to include the cost elements necessary to identify the order-filling and order-selling areas and the functional areas and tasks of marketing. It follows the structure of Exhibit 3.

It is unfortunate that many companies with highly computerized systems are working with charts of accounts designed in precomputer days. They are often inadequate, and have merely been modified for use on a computer. Marketing needs account listings tailored to its unique requirements. Some chart of accounts coding structures must be expanded from two and three digits to as many as 16 or 21 digits to accommodate the sorting requirements of marketing information. This is necessary to provide the ability to cross-code information and sort it into the information-yielding cost elements.

When information is properly assembled in the cost-revenue data bank* we should be able to get reports of the cost and income structure of a product line or the cost and income structure of responsibility centers such as territories and divisions. The concept of such an assemblage is illustrated in Exhibit 8. By cross-keying the cost/income building blocks we can develop incremental income or costs of a product, within a territory or a series of territories. We can classify the costs of programmed expense in several geographic areas and be able to sort those expenses common to a series of territories or a region.

---

*A data bank is an organized file of all of a company's pertinent marketing and financial information.

COST-SORTING CONCEPT

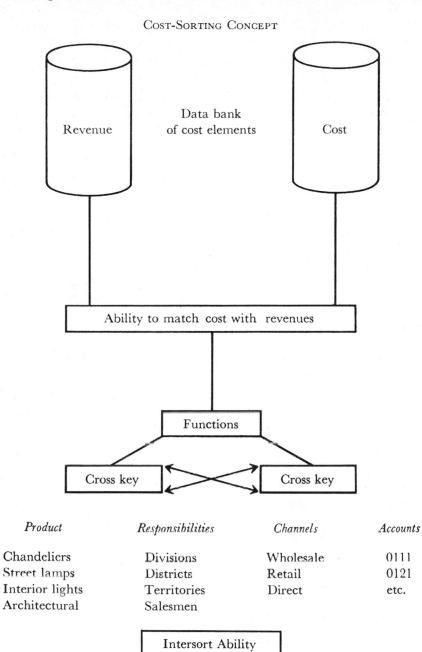

Exhibit 8

The structure portrayed here is obviously far more complex than the books kept by the Venetian trader. All of business is more complex, however. Our information systems must be responsive to the requirements of today and the future. The accounting system must produce this information in the form we need, when we need it, and accurately portray business realities. It must be done economically so that we do not hesitate to ask for necessary information.

Chapter III

Profit Concepts for Marketers

FOR SOME TIME we have been giving a series of talks at American Management Association entitled "Profit Concepts for Marketers." In these presentations we explain profit ideas that a marketer should understand to relate effectively to financial executives. In summary, these concepts are as follows:

1. Profit planning
2. Marginal costs
   a. direct costs
   b. variable costs
3. Cost elements
4. Return on investment
5. Responsibility control and reporting
6. Exception reporting
7. Integration or a management information system

These concepts of profit easily relate to marketing; they constitute the background for the profitable management of the
marketing function.

PROFIT PLANNING

Businessmen have chosen to define "profit planning" to suit
their immediate needs. Consequently, we have "customer-oriented
planning," "functional planning," and "product," "facility," personnel," and "corporate" planning. Unfortunately, many businessmen concentrate on control processes rather than on planning
procedures and react rather than initiate a long-range plan. A
plan should encompass a sufficient period for management to
control and measure performance of an "object of measurement,"
which can be a product line, a responsible person, a channel of
distribution, or an account. Unfortunately, much of the reaction
that passes as planning is based on "rolling" cycles of weeks or
months which fail to account for foreseen events. The planning
cycle must be long enough to permit evaluation of performance
under the plan and flexible enough to allow reactions to external
forces. It must consider the life of the venture and make future
projections, a process far different from budgeting.

Often budgeting is substituted for planning, which requires
goals and directions that can be defined as planning segments.
Some of these segments will be subjective. Many others, perhaps
most, should be definable and quantitative in nature. Budgeting
is reactive to planning; a series of control points are established, and
revenues, costs, and expenses are measured against the controls.

In profit planning, a planning cycle should be established.
Plans should remain stable long enough for management to determine the effectiveness of initial plans. When results are reported
against a plan, the total planning series and the prevailing assumptions should be shown in addition to forecasts revised during the
cycle. This will be illustrated in the control reports in a later chapter. The key concept for a marketer is that planning is necessary
and requires the definition of events that management has antici-
pated.

Profit planning is often formulated on a yearly basis because it occurs in a sequence that fits in the custodial accounting cycle. Planning may, however, be subdivided on a quarterly or monthly basis, or extended to five or more years.

MARGINAL COSTS

The second area to consider is that of marginal costs, and the difference between marginal and fully allocated costs. These differences were discussed in preceding chapters. The following definitions summarize the concepts involved.

Direct cost. This is a cost that occurs because a product or function exists or is contemplated. A direct cost can be identified with a product or function. It answers the question, "If the function or product were eliminated, would the cost be eliminated?" The fact that a cost is directly associated with a function or product such as manufacturing, selling, or advertising does not demarcate its performance area. Direct cost should not be confused with variable or fixed costs, terms of cost behavior that will be defined in relation to cost performance.

Indirect cost. This cost relates to the existence of several functions or products. For example, the costs of personnel who work on more than one product, such as salesmen selling a multiple product line, are indirect costs to each of the products sold. The salesmen's salaries are indirect marketing costs when a cost evaluation is made in a multiproduct line. In a manufacturing and marketing environment, the costs of corporate overhead, not directly assigned to product or cost centers, are indirect costs.

A single cost may be direct at one measurement point and indirect at a second. The determining factor is the object of measurement. If this is a product line, costs directly associated with the manufacture and sale of the product line are direct. All other costs in the business are indirect. If the object of measurement shifts to a sales territory, some of the costs of product-line measurement which were direct will remain direct costs now associated with the territory; some will become indirect; and others that were indirect will become direct. For example:

Cost	Object of Measurement	
	Product	Territory
Sales promotion display	Direct	Direct
Salesman compensation	Indirect	Direct
Product-line manager's salary	Direct	Indirect
Corporate president's salary	Indirect	Indirect

Some of the fundamental problems in management's viewing of costs occur when indirect costs are assigned to functional areas. The principles of full absorption specify that all indirect costs eventually be assigned to products. However, as will be seen in a multiproduct company, it is difficult to devise a method of assigning the indirect costs without distorting operating results.

The term "indirect" invites comparison to the direct cost structure. The term "general expense" indicates that a cost cannot be assigned to a function or product and is part of the general cost structure rather than a direct expense easily assigned.

Variable costs and cost performance. A variable cost is an expense that varies directly with volume of sales or production. As indicated earlier, costs can be variable or nonvariable (fixed). The latter cost does not vary with volume of activity, such as sales or production, and this type of fixed cost can be either programmed or standby. A programmed or managed cost is one set by management for a planning period to attain desired objectives. Examples are advertising and market research costs. A second type of nonvariable cost is a standby or capacity cost, which will not vary unless there is a drastic change in the company's operation. Some of these costs are depreciation, rent, administrative salaries, and costs that exist as long as a particular function continues. In a selling situation these would be the fixed costs of maintaining a sales office, which would be in existence only as long as needed in a sales territory plan.

Cost Building Blocks

A cost or revenue building block is the smallest element of cost or revenue that is accounted for and then assembled with other elements to represent meaningfully the cost or revenue structure of a product, product line, or responsibility center. The collection of cost and revenue building blocks starts where these elements are assembled in their smallest, most meaningful terms. This requires the ability to code units of cost or revenue that can be arranged and rearranged to conform to the varieties of information patterns required. Some of these structures are describable building blocks that can be assigned in modular form to products or responsiblity centers. An example of a module of cost is the district sales manager's salary. This is a general expense (our term for indirect) when the object of profit measurement is a product line. It is a specific expense when related to the division he manages. The ability to identify and sort the cost as both a direct and general cost results from detailed charts of accounts. These must be specifically designed to satisfy management's information needs.

The complexity of creating meaningful cost—and revenue— building blocks can be seen when, at the moment of sale, a specific cost such as a salesman's commission may be assigned to objects of measurement, such as a product, product line, distribution channel, territory, division, customer, or distributor. The information system must portray each cost element, such as commissions, into modules of direct or indirect "ownership" by function. These modules must then classify the cost to reflect behavior as either variable or fixed. Schematically, this can be shown as in Exhibit 9.

COST BEHAVIORAL BUILDING BLOCKS

Variable costs

Programmed costs ⎤
           ⎟ Depending upon object of measurement ⎡ Specific
Standby costs ⎦   ⎣ General

Exhibit 9

For an understanding of the concept of specific and general expenses and the implications of programmed and standby costs, these terms are defined and illustrated.

Specific expenses. A specific expense is one which can be identified with a specified object of profit measurement (product, territory, salesman, and so forth) under consideration; that is, the expense would not be incurred if the object were eliminated. An example of this is the product manager's salary, which would be specifically identified with the product he was managing. If the product were discontinued, the expense would be eliminated.

General expenses. A general expense is one which cannot be directly identified with a specific object of profit measurement under scrutiny; that is, the expense would not be eliminated if the given object were eliminated. An example of this involves the situation where all sales regions sell all products. The product manager's salary is not identifiable as an object of profit measurement within any of the regions. Therefore, the product manager's salary is a general expense when the object of measurement is a sales region.

It should be cautioned that the terms "specific" and "general" have meaning only in relation to the object of profit measurement under consideration. In Exhibit 10 we see the reaction to object-of-measurement changes of a merchandise manager's salary, a district sales manager's salary, advertising expense in a consumer publication, and shipping expense. Each reacts differently when we change the object of profit measurement from a product to a line responsibility.

This becomes one of the key differences between management reporting and reports resulting from traditional custodial accounting. When the object of measurement changes, the marketer requires that his information system reflect the change.

The method of accounting for an expense must be sensitive to combinations of identifiability and behavior. For example, a partially specific and partially general expense can exist; or a company may advertise a specific product and the corporate name in separate advertising programs. The expense category "advertising" probably will be partially specific and partially general when assessing product earnings.

In all programmed or standby costs under consideration, changing the object of profit measurement may or may not change whether a given expense is specific or general.

The terms "direct," "specific," "general," "variable," and "fixed costs" are classifications of cost information and are used to measure performance. To use these terms, management must also understand return on investment, responsibility and performance measurement reporting, and their integration into a management

Expense	Object of Profit Measurement	
	Product	*Division*
Merchandise manager's salary	Specific	General
District sales manager's salary	General	Specific
Consumer publication advertising	Specific	Specific
Shipping expense	General	General

Exhibit 10

information system. These are uses of cost information concepts that must be built upon a sound foundation of direct cost data where variable cost building blocks can be identified and separated from fixed and allocated expenses.

RETURN ON INVESTMENT

As early as 1917, Alfred P. Sloane, Jr., adopting techniques then in use at E. I. Dupont, recommended the use of rate of return as a decision-making tool at General Motors. In his book *My Years with General Motors*, he noted from an early report that he had written that rate of return "Enables the Corporation to direct the placing of additional capital where it will result in the greatest benefit to the Corporation as a whole." Subsequently, in a statement about the rate of return concept, he added, " . . . no other financial principle with which I am acquainted serves better than rate-of-return as an objective aid to business judgement. . . ."

Rate of return or return on investment (ROI) is the ratio of earnings to capital invested or employed in a project. (The specific computation of this ratio will be covered later.) However, it is usable in marketing planning and recently has come into use as a control device to determine acceptable levels and standards of performance. For a marketer it is usually the rate of earnings or contribution on the assets for which the marketer has responsiblity in his operation. It is used to evaluate results in a segment of the business, such as product line or project profitability.

The rate of return used in an operating area, such as marketing, is really the return on assets assigned or managed in that area or on that project. ROAM (return on assets managed) has several basic values:

- It can be related directly to the objective of the business— the return on stockholders' investment.
- It is a multifaceted computation that takes into account turnover of assets and profit margin.
- It is a tool for both planning and control to which management can easily relate.

Indeed, Sloan has stated that return on investment ". . . increases the morale of the organization by placing each operation on its own foundation, making it feel that it is part of the Corporation, assuming its own responsibility and contributing its share to the final result." It suffices that ROI is a tool worthy of consideration in managing the marketing function.

RESPONSIBILITY AND PERFORMANCE MEASUREMENT REPORTING

An organization chart generally portrays the line and staff responsibilities within a company for revenues, costs, and profit. The accounting structure of an organization should fit the responsibility reporting requirements so that performance can be measured, grouping results with individual responsibilities. The reporting structure should be so structured that the president of an organization, upon receiving his performance report package, can easily identify the persons responsible for specific areas and performance variances.

In performance measurement reporting, the marketing report structure should clearly identify the costs of order getting and those of order filling. The division of labor and responsibility between the functional groupings enables the marketing manager to identify those specific areas of either sales effort or distribution that require attention. A reporting system that does not segregate information into responsible groupings will tend to bury costs in such a manner that inefficiencies can be hidden, while excellent performance can go unnoticed.

EXCEPTION REPORTING

With the advent of the computer it has become possible to rapidly focus reporting effort and managerial attention on specific areas. The computer can generate overwhelming quantities of data, much of which does not require a manager's attention. Many managers, however, receive voluminous amounts of computer printouts each month which they neither use nor read. For data of this sort to be useful, the reports are culled for pertinent information and compiled into smaller reports. This is actually duplication of effort—the effort to produce the data and the second effort to realign the data into a form usable by management can both be done more efficiently by a computer. The computer can be programmed to sort the information according to preset parameters and highlight those exception situations requiring management attention.

Exception reporting is the display of those figures that deviate from plan, or that are, in accounting terms, "at variance." Of course, this requires that a plan exist at each of the reporting levels. Exception reporting allows the computer to do the sorting and identifying in situations requiring action. The simplest example of an exception report is a "no sales" report by customer name. This causes customers to be reported as a "no sale" to the salesman and the sales manager. Another exception report would show the situations where costs are exceeding budget.

Exception reporting is a time-saving tool easily accomplished by modern computer programming. However, the concept is not necessarily limited to the computer. In smaller companies or work units, clerks can be held responsible for reporting variations from plans, and marketing managers can specify those deviations from approved performance that they want called to their attention.

Other terms that require definition and that will be covered are profit contribution, gross profit, marketing costs and variances, standard costs, cost center, and sensitivity.

Profit contribution. This is the difference between sales and all variable costs regardless of whether the latter originate in a manufacturing, selling, or administrative function.

Gross profit. This is the difference between sales and all manufacturing costs regardless of whether the latter are variable or fixed.

Marketing costs and variances. Marketing costs are all those business expenses that arise from making goods available for sale. These costs must be identified for the planning and control of the marketing function. In order for the marketer to evaluate deviations from plan, he must first work within a plan where standards of performance are determined. Once these are available, actual market performance can be measured and checked against the standards. The marketer can then isolate the variances from expected performance and can seek methods to improve the performance. Utilizing the profitability concepts discussed, a marketer can control his performance by utilizing the four variances: volume, mix, price, and budget.

Volume variance. This is the effect on profit of deviations from planned volumes of sales. It is the variance from standard profit contribution that occurs because of variances from planned sales. In many operations, where inadequate management information exists, the volume variance is merely an expression of sales efficiency, expressed in units or dollars of sales without carrying it to the next step, which is its effect on profit.

Mix variance. This is the effect on profit of deviation from the planned mix of sales. This is the variance in standard profit contribution caused by actual sales ratios that are different than planned ratios (mix) in products or product lines with differing contribution rates. The mix variance is one of the most overlooked, underused, and rarely understood variances in modern marketing.

Price variance. This is the effect on profit resulting from deviations from established selling prices after allowances are made for normal discounts and any planned price concessions. This variance is easily understood and can quickly be obtained by subtracting actual sales volume at actual prices from actual sales at planned or standard selling prices.

When a marketer has price, volume, and mix variances for the many components of his business, whether it be by product line, region, or sales territory, he possesses the tools for rapid market analysis. He can isolate those reasons for major deviations from plan.

Budget variance. This is the effect on profit of variations from standard or budgeted costs or allowances. It is a common variance and includes the variances from planned sales deductions such as cash discounts, sales commissions, and freight. It also includes variations from programmed costs in such areas as compensation, advertising, sales promotion, and research. In the manufacturing process, it includes departmental spending variances such as material usage, labor efficiency, and overhead expense.

There are several other terms that should be defined. These will form the structure of the systems that will be discussed in later chapters. These terms are:

Standard unit. This is an authorized planned measure of time or quantity per unit of work done or result achieved, a desired attainment; for example, the number of minutes allowed to produce a stamping or to type an invoice, or the amount of raw materials allowed per unit of product.

Standard cost. This is the expected cost to manufacture or market a product.

Standard unit cost. This is a standard expressed in terms of planned cost dollars. The term generally applies to unit of product, but may sometimes be used to refer to such things as allowable costs per machine hour.

Gross standard profit contribution. This is a profit contribution to be generated by the sale or production of all units of product at the planned standard cost.

Cost center. This is usually an area in which work is done and in which identified costs are incurred under executive control. In other words, it is any division, department, subdivision, or any other unit of activity into which a manufacturing unit and its operations are divided for purposes of cost assignment. A profit center, however, is a performance measurement responsibility center such as the marketing function or certain types of selling activity, for example, a wholesale sales division. In these areas there are revenue and costs.

Sensitivity. This is a degree to which a decision can become critical if there are changes in the magnitude of the data on which the decision is based. Sensitivity is also, in a profit sense, the degree to which profits will be affected by a change in one of the cost or revenue elements.

One of the best arguments for conversion of a full absorption management reporting system to direct costing principles is the sensitivity of certain multiproduct, product-line divisions. Where a company has one product there is no problem of allocation rates. In effect a one-product company is on a direct cost system. However, as a company becomes complex and has more products and more product lines, absorption rate distortions can portray products as net loss products that in reality contribute to profits. The degree of sensitivity of a product to this profit contribution distortion will depend upon its rate of overhead absorption.

THE MANAGEMENT INFORMATION SYSTEM

The concepts expressed in this chapter form the components of a management information system, which should have the following characteristics:

- The information necessary for planning and decision making.
- A stratified reporting structure tailored to specific management needs.
- A responsive cost system.

The purpose of a management information system is to save management time by presenting the information necessary to run the company and measure performance. In order to be of value it must be timely, accurate, and sensitive to business conditions.

The design and structuring of management information systems has become a fine art. In recent years, it has been the subject of numerous articles and books. It has also become an extremely important assignment within many corporations at the vice-presidential level. Today the title "Vice President for Management Information" is common. Ten to fifteen years ago it was unknown.

In marketing, the information needs of each company will differ. Some of these needs can only be decided upon after exhaustive and intensive study. The structuring of this information system, starting with the underlying cost concepts and resulting in the final portrayal of a structured system of reports, will be the subject of following chapters.

Chapter IV

Product Line Profitability

To ILLUSTRATE how marketing cost behavior and the needs of a marketing information system differ from custodial accounting concepts, we will use the case of the Badger Light Company. The difference between custodial and management accounting will be illustrated, and the uses of management accounting will be discussed.

THE CORPORATE HISTORY

The Badger Light Company started as a small, family-owned manufacturing firm. Its first main product line was desk lamps, a line that grew rapidly during the early days of the company.

In 1923 the son of the founder joined the firm and broadened its design and manufacturing capability by servicing architects on a design-to-order basis. His wife, a commercial artist before mar-

47

riage, developed a highly stylized line of residential light fixtures that were popular and contributed to company growth during the 1930's.

With World War II the company expanded into the commercial lighting field and established an industrial division. By the early sixties the firm had over 24 million dollars of sales a year and national distribution of its products.

In 1962, to resolve potential estate problems and to provide an incentive base for professional management, the company sold stock to the public. The family retained control, however, by retaining about 60 percent of total stock.

The Badger Light Company now manufactures and distributes approximately 350 varieties of fluorescent and incandescent light fixtures for residential, architectural, and industrial distribution. It has manufacturing facilities and five regional warehouses to supply its sales requirements, solely in the domestic market.

The company's executive offices are located in a large midwestern city, and the manufacturing plants are geographically dispersed. Total corporate employment is about 1,100 persons.

THE MARKETING STRUCTURE

The company manufactures approximately 350 varieties of lighting fixtures. These products may be divided into three product lines:

1. Residential Group
   a. Chandeliers
   b. Spotlights
   c. Close-to-wall fixtures
   d. Outdoor fixtures
2. Architectural Group
   a. Circular recessed fixtures
   b. Commercial spotlights
   c. Recessed fluorescent fixtures
   d. Commercial wall fixtures
3. Industrial Group
   a. Fluorescent fixtures
   b. Street lighting fixtures

CHANNELS OF DISTRIBUTION

The company's products are sold through two channels of distribution, wholesale and contract. Each of these channels constitutes a division for purposes of internal reporting.

The wholesale division. The company distributes about three-quarters of its annual sales through a network of about 475 electrical supply houses and home lighting distributors. Internally, the company has divided the United States into eight sales districts, each supervised by a district sales manager who has between three and ten salesmen reporting to him. The salesmen are responsible for both servicing the distributors in their area and creating business by independent contact. Sales by independent contact are filled through an area distributor of the customer's choice. A sales office is located in each district.

The contract division. The remaining 25 percent of sales are made through the contract division, headquartered in the corporate executive offices and responsible for all sealed bidding. The bids originate with governmental bodies, certain industrial customers, and a small number of architectural engineering firms. A sales force of six men develops and services the contract business. This division sets its own price policy.

CORPORATE MARKETING ORGANIZATION

The corporate marketing organization of the Badger Light Company is illustrated in Exhibits 11, 12, and 13. Product managers are responsible for establishing and coordinating all facets of the marketing effort pertaining to their product groups. They set list pricing policy and sales forecast. Prices differing from list must have the merchandising manager's approval.

Those reporting to the vice president for sales are responsible for implementing the marketing effort established by the merchandising group. Each district sales manager prepares a sales forecast, coordinated with that developed by the merchandising organization. The product styling group is responsible for continuing style and engineering innovation in existing product lines and for research and development of new product lines.

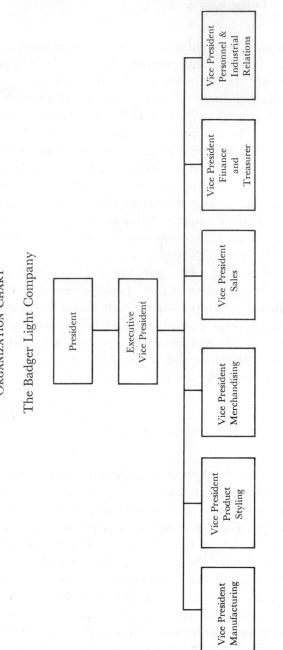

ORGANIZATION CHART

The Badger Light Company

President

Executive
Vice President

Vice President
Manufacturing

Vice President
Product
Styling

Vice President
Merchandising

Vice President
Sales

Vice President
Finance
and
Treasurer

Vice President
Personnel &
Industrial
Relations

Exhibit 11

ORGANIZATION CHART—MANUFACTURING AND FINANCE

The Badger Light Company

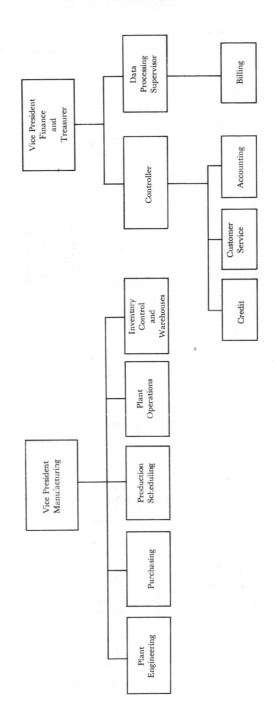

Exhibit 12

ORGANIZATION CHART—MARKETING

The Badger Light Company

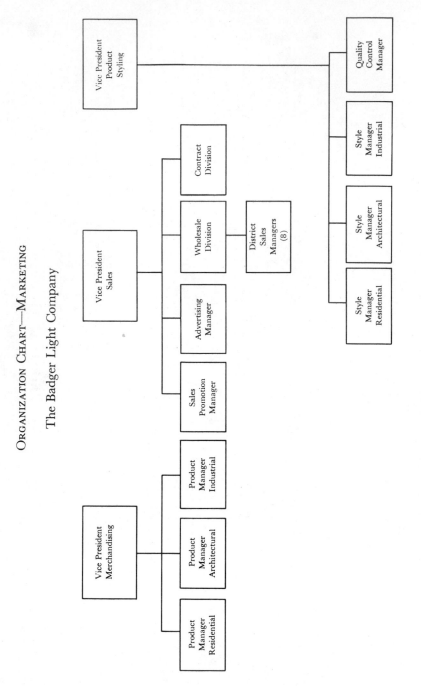

Exhibit 13

The company's organization chart for manufacturing and finance is shown in Exhibit 12. This is presented so that the origin of reports and information can be shown. The corporate controller supervises the accounting function, reporting to the vice president of finance and the treasurer of the company, while the data processing supervisor is in charge of the corporate billing process. This is necessary information, since the control of the order entry and billing systems, the source of much marketing information, and the financial data of the company are in the hands of two nonmarketing functions, the Controller's office and the data processing group.

The competitive factor. Each of the firm's products is in the top price bracket of its respective line. The company stresses the engineering and esthetic qualities of its products, being concerned with such factors as lighting and electrical efficiency, ease of installation and servicing, dependability of construction materials, and fixture appearance relative to interior design.

The company has over 15 prime competitors, no one of which dominates the quality fixture field. There are lower-price, non-specification quality manufacturers, probably in the hundreds. They are characterized by factors such as limited geographical sales scope, a single manufacturing facility, and annual sales of less than $500,000. None of the lower-price manufacturers has been a factor in the quality lighting national market.

Advertising and promotion. The company advertises in consumer, trade, professional, and industrial publications. Publications selected are consistent with the company's high-quality, top-price marketing strategy. The company has no cooperative advertising program and grants no discounts except for payment within ten days.

Direct mailings are utilized extensively to reach architects, engineers, residential contractors, industrial purchasing agents, and governmental agencies.

The company conducts training programs for its distributors and distributor salesmen. Product characteristics, interior design considerations, and personal selling techniques are stressed in these sales programs.

Market research. The company does not have the advantage of estimates of market potential or market penetration. None of the industry's trade associations accumulate such data, and no reporting service similar to a Nielsen Data Service exists. The company relies on salesmen's feedback, contacts with competitors, and association meetings for a feel of its position within the market.

Compensation of salesmen. In terms of compensation plans, the company has two types of salesmen, full-line and contract salesmen. The former sells residential, commercial, and industrial fixtures. He receives a percentage compensation which differs with each product line. This type of salesman receives no salary. A contract salesman is salaried and services bid, house, and special accounts.

THE BADGER LIGHT COMPANY SITUATION

The executive vice president of this firm was new to the company. He was attracted to it from a job in a smaller, privately held lighting concern that concentrated on styling of higher priced residential lighting fixtures. He knew of Badger Light as a progressive, financially well-structured company. Prior to taking the job, he had seen the balance sheet and statement of earnings for the preceding year. These are shown in Exhibits 14 and 15. He was impressed by the fact that the net earnings of the company were about 6.7 percent of sales before taxes and that the gross profit percentage of 34.8 percent compared favorably to what he had experienced in the fashion fixture business.

Consequently, upon arrival at Badger Light Company, he was puzzled by the product group earnings statement that he received from the controller. This is shown in Exhibit 16. He knew that the firm's industrial products carried lower margins than either the residential or architectural lines, but was shocked to learn that the group's loss had widened to over one million dollars in the face of a 20 percent sales increase. Also, having recently completed a tour of all the wholesale division offices, the executive vice president was anxious to examine their relative profitability. Such information, however, did not seem to be readily available. Accordingly, he undertook to examine the company's expenses and organization in an effort to determine how he should judge profitability and assign employee responsibility.

STATEMENT OF FINANCIAL POSITION
The Badger Light Company
Year Ended December 31, 1968

Assets

Current assets	
Cash	$ 756,427
Accounts receivable	6,322,113
Inventories	7,144,567
Prepaid expenses	637,521
Total current assets	$14,860,628
Property, plant, and equipment	3,426,531
Other investments	1,050,000
Other assets	934,621
	$20,271,780

Liabilities and Owners' Equity

Current liabilities	
Trade accounts payable	$ 2,321,333
Accrued wages and salaries	647,821
Federal income taxes payable	1,473,198
Other liabilities	693,114
Total current liabilities	$ 5,135,466
Stockholders' equity	
Common stock	1,200,000
Retained earnings	13,936,314
	$20,271,780

Exhibit 14

STATEMENT OF EARNINGS
The Badger Light Company
Year Ended December 31, 1968
(000's omitted)

			%
Net sales		$27,030	100.0
Cost of sales			
Direct material	$11,909		
Direct labor	1,870		
Manufacturing overhead	3,834	17,613	
Gross profit		$ 9,417	34.8
Selling expenses			
Salaries	$ 2,810		
Advertising and promotion	1,004		
Shipping	882		
Other	1,093		
	$ 5,789		
General and administrative expenses	1,818	7,607	
Earnings before taxes		$ 1,810	6.7
Provision for taxes		869	
Net earnings		$ 941	3.5

Exhibit 15

The custodial statement of product line profit. The product line earnings statement presented to the executive vice president by the controller is shown in Exhibit 16. By questioning the controller, he ascertained that the figures within the statement were based upon full allocation of costs to the product lines, as in the corporate custodial accounting statement. The costs assigned to each product group were most often allocated on the basis of sales, in order to allocate fully the dollars of expense found in any natural account

STATEMENT OF EARNINGS BY PRODUCT GROUP
The Badger Light Company
Year Ended December 31, 1968
(000's omitted)

	Total Company	(Residential)	Product Group (Architec- tural)	(Industrial)
Net sales	$27,030	$4,550	$18,228	$ 4,252
Cost of sales				
Direct materials	$11,909	$1,805	$ 7,059	$ 3,045
Direct labor	1,870	277	1,229	364
Manufacturing overhead	3,834	412	2,533	889
	$17,613	$2,494	$10,821	$ 4,298
Gross profit	$ 9,417	$2,056	$ 7,407	$ (46)
Percentage	34.8	45.3	40.6	(1.1)
Selling expenses				
Salaries	$ 2,810	$ 343	$ 2,010	$ 457
Advertising and promotion	1,004	240	714	50
Shipping	882	150	595	137
Other	1,093	211	823	59
	$ 5,789	$ 944	$ 4,142	$ 703
General and administrative expenses	$ 1,818	$ 309	$ 1,227	$ 282
Earnings before taxes	$ 1,810	$ 803	$ 2,038	$(1,031)
Percentage	6.7	17.7	11.2	(24.2)
Provision for taxes	869			
Net earnings	$ 941			

Exhibit 16

classification. Accordingly, it appears that the industrial product group is unprofitable.

The industrial product group shows a loss of $1,031,000 after general and administrative expenses of $282,000 and selling expenses of $703,000 were added to a gross loss of $46,000. This gross loss of $46,000 attracted the notice of the executive vice president first, since it appeared that the line was not contributing toward selling and G & A expenses. By questioning the loss, he determined that the $889,000 manufacturing overhead consisted of both direct and allocated overhead assigned to the product group. These allocations did not necessarily reflect costs that were directly assignable to the products' existence. In other words, if the decision were made to eliminate the industrial product group, the $889,000 manufacturing overhead would not be eliminated, and the company would not necessarily realize a savings of the $46,000 loss indicated as a gross loss for the product group.

Gross profit and profit contribution. In order to understand the implications of using a fully allocated product line statement (Exhibit 15) for decision making, the executive vice president had to understand the difference between the concepts of gross profit and profit contribution. Gross profit (or gross margin or gross income) is a meaningful custodial accounting term. It is the difference between sales and "cost of sales." In the "cost of sales" (or "cost of goods sold") are encompassed all items included in the accountant's concept of "cost of sales." These costs are all the "matched" or "inventoried" costs of manufacture that can be attributed to the "income stream" or revenue that will come from the sale. As we have discerned, this is a custodial costing concept. In an accounting sense, the cost of goods sold contains *all* costs of doing business that can conceivably be attributed to that sale. Since it contains all manufacturing costs that can conceivably be attributed, it is a fully absorbed cost of goods sold. Other costs which are not matchable are not included, but are shown as selling or general and administrative costs.

On the other hand, profit contribution is defined as the revenue from a sale less the incremental or variable costs. Profit contribution is a concept that at the outset takes into account the variability of cost performance. With this concept the marginal income from each sale is shown. Only those direct costs which are attributable to the sale are assigned. Only the incremental costs of the sale are deducted from revenue to arrive at profit contribution. To repeat, these costs are:

- Specific sales deductions, such as cash discounts, trade discounts, sales commissions, and freight out, which are non-inventoriable costs specifically incurred as the result of a sale.

- Specification costs for direct material and direct labor. They are inventoriable costs which are specifically identified with a unit of product in standard amounts which are obtained from bills of material and process routing sheets.
- Variable overhead, which includes all normal recurring costs not specifically identifiable with an individual unit of product but varying in some manner with volume.

Under a profit contribution system, a break-even volume for a product or product line can be computed and defined. A break-even point is that point at which the accumulated profit contribution from units sold equals the standby and programmed costs. Profit contribution is a marginal income concept. It is the first level of profitability generated by sales in units being assigned direct unit attributable costs. A profit contribution reoccurs for each unit of product sold.

In a comparison of a profit contribution statement and a fully absorbed statement, the sales dollar value and the net profit figures will be identical, assuming that the dollar values of the beginning and ending inventories are identical.

Since the executive vice president needed these accounting statements for decision-making purposes about the product lines of his company, he had to isolate costs for each of the marketing and distribution functions within the firm. In order to do this, he had the costs divided within Badger Light into order-getting and order-filling costs. The division of these costs is illustrated in Exhibit 18. Included in this breakdown are costs that were shown in the fully allocated statement as applicable to the "selling" and "general and administrative" functions. The breakdown of these costs is shown in Exhibits 18 and 19.

This breakdown of order-filling and order-getting costs, as shown in Exhibit 18, indicates the necessary detail that should be available in a modern, marketing-oriented chart of accounts. The executive vice president was fortunate that the Badger Light Company's chart of accounts had the necessary detail available for his analysis.

Results of the executive vice president's examination. The examination disclosed facts such as those mentioned on page 63.

DISTRIBUTION COSTS BY FUNCTION
The Badger Light Company
(000's omitted)

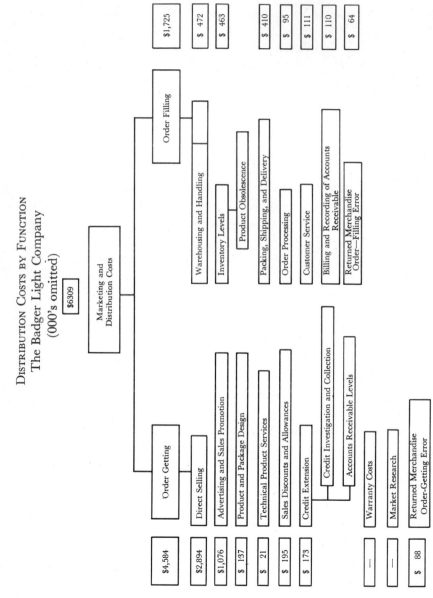

Exhibit 17

Schedule of Selling Expenses
The Badger Light Company
Year Ended December 31, 1968
(000's omitted)

Salaries		
Salesmen's compensation		
Commissions	$1,461	
Prizes and awards	190	
Sales and merchandising		
District sales managers	386	
Merchandising managers	102	
Styling managers	137	
Advertising	72	
Sales offices	243	
Drafting	76	
Contract	143	$2,810
Advertising and promotion		
Advertising		
Consumer publications	$ 360	
Trade, professional, and industrial publications	194	
Catalogs and price lists	214	
Direct mail circulars	75	
Displays	35	
Promotion		
Shows	39	
Distributor training	51	
Salesmen's samples	36	1,004
Shipping expenses		
Wages and salaries	$ 475	
Rentals and depreciation	211	
Supplies and maintenance	196	882
Other selling expenses		
Sales offices	$ 210	
Sales discounts	195	
Markdowns on finished goods	430	
Travel and entertainment	106	
Cost of returns	152	1,093
Total selling expenses		$5,789

Exhibit 18

Schedule of General and Administrative Expenses
The Badger Light Company
Year Ended December 31, 1968
(000's omitted)

	Total	Marketing and Distribution Costs
Salaries		
Executive staff	$ 490	$ 83
Controller's staff	64	—
Systems group	84	17
Credit and accounts receivable	91	91
Data processing	135	19
Billing supervisor and clerks	32	32
Order control and processing	31	31
Phone operators and office boys	21	—
Other Expenses		
Postage	46	—
Stationery and supplies	125	56
Telephone and telegraph	37	—
Credit rating bureau	9	9
Trade associations	11	5
Rental of data processing equipment	183	—
Repairs	13	—
Travel expense	47	21
Professional fees	164	27
Insurance	14	—
State and local taxes	56	33
Contributions	51	—
Bad debts	96	96
Depreciation	9	—
	$1,818	

Distribution costs included in general and administrative expenses	$ 520
Selling expenses	5,789
Total distribution costs	$6,309

Exhibit 19

- Certain of the manufacturing, selling, and general administrative expenses appeared to vary with sales while others did not.
- Certain of the selling, general, and administrative expenses appeared to be connected with only one of the company's sales divisions; some appeared to be connected with a single product group.
- The wholesale division's eight field sales offices were the object of spending in excess of $800,000. This spending was broken down as:

District sales managers	$386,000
Sales office salaries	243,000
Sales office expense	210,000
	$839,000

- Advertising and publications expense aggregated $554,000, of which $360,000 was specifically spent for the residential product group.
- Markdowns on product lines totaled $430,000.

These facts were unavailable on the basis of the information shown in Exhibit 16. The indicated gross loss of the industrial product line did not show that this product line was making a contribution toward the fixed costs of the company. As a product line it contributes $160,000 to support the firm's general standby and programmed expenses. This is shown in Exhibits 20 and 21, a statement of earnings by product, constructed on a marginal format.

In this format we see that the industrial product line:

- Contributed $160,000 to general standby and programmed expense.
- Contributed $.098 of each dollar of sales toward its non-variable specific product expense structure.
- Contributed $422,000 toward its specific standby and programmed product expenses, which were $262,000.

STATEMENT OF EARNINGS BY PRODUCT
The Badger Light Company
Year Ended December 31, 1968
(000's omitted)

		Product		
	Total Company	Resi- dential	Archi- tectural	Industrial
Gross sales	$27,240	$4,560	$18,398	$4,282
Variable costs	17,338	2,630	10,848	3,860
Profit contribution	9,902	1,930	7,550	422
Profit contribution percentage	36.3%	42.4%	41.0%	9.8%
*Specific product expenses	2,090	1,028	800	262
Product earnings	7,812	$ 902	$ 6,750	$ 160
*General expenses	6,002			
Earnings before taxes	$ 1,810			

*Specific and general expenses include standby and programmed costs.

Exhibit 20

The specific expenses identifiable to each product line are assigned to product lines in Exhibit 20. In this exhibit, all variable costs of selling, manufacturing, and administration are subtracted from gross sales. In place of gross profit, product profit contribution is reflected. The expenses identifiable to each product line are deducted from each category to arrive at a product group earnings figure. The remaining expenses, those which cannot be allocated to any specific product line, are displayed as general expenses attributable to the total company instead of allocating them to all product lines. Without arbitrary allocations, management is able to review the relative profitability of each product line. Management can plan the product group contribution necessary to cover the general expense structure.

By using this format of reporting, management can manage the relative profitability of each product line. With variable costs separated from nonvariable costs, management can see the effects

Detail for Exhibit 20

STATEMENT OF EARNINGS BY PRODUCT

The Badger Light Company

Year Ended December 31, 1968

(000's omitted)

	Total Company	Per Unit						Product			
			Residential	Per Unit	Architectural	Per Unit	Industrial
Gross sales	$27,240	$50.70	$4,560	$183.98	$18,389	$24.47	$4,282
Variable costs							
Specific sales deductions							
Cash discounts allowed	195		25		127		43
Commissions	1,461		225		1,184		52
Trade discounts	210		10		170		30
Direct materials	11,909		1,805		7,059		3,045
Direct labor	1,870		277		1,229		364
Variable manufacturing overhead	1,140		167		694		279
Variable selling	448		81		330		37
Variable administration	105		40		55		10
Total variable costs	17,338	29.20	2,630	108.48	10,848	22.03	3,860
Profit contribution	9,902	$21.50	1,930	$ 75.50	7,550	$ 2.44	422
	36.3%		42.4%		41.0%		9.8%
Specific product expenses							
Selling							
Prizes and awards	35		8		23		4
Merchandising managers	102		34		43		25
Styling managers	114		38		43		33
Advertising managers	58		27		27		4
Drafting	43		—		41		2
Contract	101		—		78		23
Consumer publications	360		360		—		—
Trade, professional, and industrial publications	194		—		151		43

Exhibit 21 (continued on page 66)

Detail for Exhibit 20 (Continued)

	Total Company		Product			
		Per Unit	Residential	Per Unit	Architectural	Per Unit	Industrial
Catalogs and price lists	214		114		48		52
Direct mail circulars	75		—		43		32
Displays	35		10		25		—
Shows	27		6		12		9
Salesmen's samples	36		21		10		5
Markdowns on finished goods	430		280		140		10
Travel and entertainment	34		6		12		16
Cost of returns	152		97		53		2
Total	2,010		1,001		749		260
Administrative							
Trade associations	5		3		1		1
Travel expense	21		—		21		—
Professional fees	27		24		3		—
Provision for doubtful accounts	27		—		26		1
Total	80		27		51		2
Total specific expenses	2,090		1,028		800		262
Product earnings	7,812		$ 902		$ 6,750		$ 160
Product earnings—index	0.79		0.47		0.90		0.38
General expenses							
Selling	1,675						
Administrative	1,633						
Manufacturing	2,694						
	6,002						
Earnings before taxes	$1,810						

Exhibit 21

of increased volume or a change in prices. Using this profitability analysis, the executive vice president was able to observe the three product lines and see that in the industrial product group, he had 9.8 percent profit contribution toward specific product expenses, the lowest contribution of the three product lines. He was able to see that the industrial product lines required further analysis.

To illustrate the type of analysis the industrial division requires, we have selected the residential product line and will later analyze the industrial. The residential product line appears to be quite healthy. Using these concepts, we can dissect and probe into this product line and see whether there are any weak spots.

In Exhibits 22 and 23, figures are shown for the residential product line, which consists of chandeliers, spotlights, close-to-wall fixtures, and outdoor fixtures. An analysis indicates that chandeliers have the weakest profit position, even though their sales are close

RESIDENTIAL PRODUCT GROUP EARNINGS
The Badger Light Company
(000's omitted)

	Total Residential Group	Product Line			
		Chande- liers	Spot- lights	Close-to- Wall Fixtures	Outdoor Fixtures
Gross sales	$4,560	$1,110	$1,413	$1,483	$554
Variable costs	2,630	885	639	786	320
Profit contribution	1,930	225	774	697	234
Profit contribution percentage	42.4%	20.2%	54.8%	47.0%	42.3%
Specific product line expenses	849	336	68	285	160
Product line earnings (loss)	1,081	$(111)	$ 706	$ 412	$ 74
*Product line earnings index	0.56	(0.49)	0.91	0.59	0.32
General product line expenses	179				
Residential product group earnings	$ 902				

*Product line earnings index portrays the relationship of profit contribution to the specific standby and programmed product line expenses in ratio form. It is a tool of analysis, but because it combines standby and programmed costs in the ratio, it is of limited use in forecasting future relationships in a dynamic situation.

Exhibit 22

Detail for Exhibit 22
STATEMENT OF PRODUCT EARNINGS, RESIDENTIAL GROUP
The Badger Light Company
Year Ended December 31, 1968
(000's omitted)

	Total Residential Group	Product Line			
		Chandeliers	Spotlights	Close-to-Wall Fixtures	Outdoor Fixtures
Gross sales	$4,560	$1,110	$1,413	$1,483	$554
Variable costs					
Specific sales deductions					
Cash discounts allowed	25	6	8	8	3
Commissions	225	78	56	58	33
Trade discounts	10	3	3	3	1
Direct materials	805	588	433	574	210
Direct labor	277	105	70	63	39
Variable manufacturing overhead	167	42	56	55	14
Variable selling and administrative	121	63	13	25	20
Profit contribution	930	225	774	697	234
Profit contribution percentage	42.4%	20.2%	54.8%	47.0%	42.3%
Specific product line expenses					
Selling					
Advertising salaries	27	23	—	4	—
Consumer publications	300	130	30	100	40
Catalogs and price lists	100	40	5	30	25
Salesmen's samples	21	—	6	15	—
Markdowns	280	100	25	115	40
Cost of returns	97	43	2	21	31
Administrative					
Professional fees	24	—	—	—	24
Product line earnings	1,081	$ (111)	$ 706	$ 412	$ 74
Product line earnings— index	0.56	(0.49)	0.91	0.59	0.32
General product line expenses					
Selling—compensation					
Prizes and awards	8				
Merchandise managers	34				
Styling managers	38				

Selling—advertising and
promotion

Consumer publications	60
Catalogs and price lists	14
Shows	6
Displays	10

Selling—other

Travel and

entertainment	6

Administrative

Trade associations	3

Residential product group earnings	$ 902

Exhibit 23

ARCHITECTURAL PRODUCT GROUP EARNINGS
The Badger Light Company
Year Ended December 31, 1968
(000's omitted)

			Product Line		
	Total Archi- tectural Group	Circular Recessed	Com- mercial Spot- lights	Rectan- gular Fluo- rescent	Com- mercial Wall Fixtures
Gross sales	$18,398	$3,513	$1,297	$11,361	$2,227
Variable costs	10,848	1,794	707	7,139	1,208
Profit contribution	7,550	1,719	590	4,222	1,019
Profit contribution percentage	41.0%	49.0%	45.5%	37.2%	48.0%
Specific product line expenses	411	69	87	203	52
Product line earnings	7,139	$1,650	$ 503	$ 4,019	$ 967
Product line earnings— index	0.95	0.96	0.85	0.95	0.95
General product line expenses	389				
Architectural product group earnings	$ 6,750				

Exhibit 24

to the highest in the line. Further analysis indicates that chandeliers' profit contribution is the line's lowest and that their specific product line expenses are the highest. The combination of low profit contribution and high product line expenses results in a loss position for the product.

What kind of questions can management ask at this point? Perhaps the selling efforts are misdirected in this product line, and sales effort should be directed toward the other three product groups, which have higher profit contributions (see Exhibits 22 and 23). Or perhaps management is allocating too much advertising expense to chandeliers. A market position analysis may dictate that this profit picture is reasonable, and chandeliers are a "loss leader," carrying the line and carrying the prestige of the residential group.

Detail for Exhibit 24
STATEMENT OF PRODUCT EARNINGS, ARCHITECTURAL GROUP
The Badger Light Company
Year Ended December 31, 1968
(000's omitted)

		Product Line			
	Total Architectural Group	Circular Recessed	Commercial Spotlights	Rectangular Fluorescent	Commercial Wall Fixtures
Gross sales	$18,398	$3,513	$1,297	$11,361	$2,227
Variable costs					
Specific sales deduction					
Cash discounts allowed	127	21	9	80	17
Commissions	1,184	140	105	894	45
Trade discounts	170	10	10	140	10
Direct materials	7,059	1,138	381	4,661	879
Direct labor	1,229	261	80	752	136
Variable manufacturing overhead	694	162	41	451	40
Variable selling and administrative	385	62	81	161	81
Profit contribution	7,550	1,719	590	4,222	1,019
Profit contribution percentage	41.0%	49.0%	45.5%	37.2%	45.8%

Specific product line
   expenses
  Selling

Prizes and awards	13	—	13	—	—
Advertising salaries	27	—	27	—	—
Trade, professional, and industrial publications	104	3	20	75	6
Catalogs and price lists	40	5	8	20	7
Salesmen's samples	10	1	4	4	1
Markdowns	140	50	10	60	20
Cost of returns	53	10	5	20	18
Administrative					
Travel expense	21	—	—	—	—
Professional fee	3	—	—	—	—
Product line earnings	7,139	$1,650	$ 503	$ 4,019	$ 967
Product line earnings— index	0.95	0.96	0.85	0.95	0.95

General product group
   expenses
  Selling—compensation

Prizes and awards	10
Merchandising manager	43
Styling manager	43
Drafting	41
Contract	78
Trade, professional, and industrial publications	47
Catalogs and price lists	8
Direct mail circulars	43
Displays	25
Shows	12
Travel and entertainment	12
Administrative	
Trade associations	1
Bad debts	26
Architectural product group earnings	$ 6,750

Exhibit 25

Indeed, an analysis of specific product line expenses, particularly those of selling in this company, indicated that more than one-third of the advertising burden of the product line was being carried by chandeliers, which were the "high-fashion" and "prestige" leaders that spearheaded the firm's marketing plan. What was startling was the indication that this particular product had a disproportionate share of markdowns and returns. An analysis of the markdown and return figures (see Exhibit 23) indicated that $143,000 was lost in markdowns and returns. By analyzing reasons for markdowns and returns, the executive vice president and management were able to bring these figures in line. The financial analysis was able to portray a return situation that management otherwise had not been aware existed.

The industrial product line. Analysis of the industrial product line (see Exhibits 26 and 27) indicates that this product line consists of two product groups: fluorescent fixtures and street lights. Flu-

INDUSTRIAL PRODUCT GROUP EARNINGS
The Badger Light Company
Year Ended December 31, 1968
(000's omitted)

	Total Industrial Group	Product Lines	
		Fluorescent	Street Lights
Gross sales	$4,282	$2,444	$1,838
Variable costs	3,860	2,083	1,777
Profit contribution	422	361	61
Profit contribution percentage	9.8%	14.8%	3.3%
Specific product line expenses	204	105	99
Product line earnings (loss)	218	$ 256	$ (38)
Product line earnings index	0.52	0.71	(0.62)
General product line expenses	58		
Industrial product group earnings	$ 160		

Exhibit 26

The Badger Light Company
Year Ended December 31, 1968
(000's omitted)

	Total Industrial Group	Product Lines	
		Fluorescent	Street Lights
Gross sales	$4,287	$2,444	$1,838
Variable costs			
Specific sales deductions			
Cash discounts allowed	43	43	—
Commissions	52	52	—
Trade discounts	30	30	—
Direct materials	3,045	1,519	1,526
Direct labor	364	210	154
Variable manufacturing overhead	279	209	70
Variable selling and administrative	47	20	27
Profit contribution	422	361	61
Profit contribution percentage	9.8%	14.8%	3.3%
Specific product line expenses			
Selling—compensation			
Prizes and awards	4	4	—
Advertising salaries	4	2	2
Drafting	2	—	2
Contract	23	5	18
Selling—advertising and promotion			
Trade, professional, and industrial			
publications	43	25	18
Catalogs and price lists	52	15	37
Direct mail circulars	32	18	14
Shows	9	9	
Salesmen's samples	5	3	2
Selling—other			
Markdowns	10	10	—
Travel and entertainment	16	11	5
Cost of returns	2	1	1
Administrative			
Trade associations	1	1	—
Provision for doubtful accounts	1	1	—
Product line earnings (loss)	218	$ 256	$ (38)
Product line earnings index	0.52	0.71	(0.62)
General product line expenses			
Merchandise manager's salary	25		
Styling manager's salary	33		
Industrial product group earnings	$ 160		

Exhibit 27

orescent fixtures had product line earnings of $256,000, while
street lights had product line losses of $38,000. Street lights con-
tributed 3.3 percent on sales, but the specific standby and programmed expenses were greater than the total profit contribution.
In order to determine the reason for this, a detailed analysis was
made (see Exhibit 27). It was determined that, in addition to a
low profit contribution percentage, the costs of contract selling,
trade, professional, and industrial publication advertising, and
catalogs, price lists, and direct mail circulars accounted for more
than twice the amount of money lost in the product line. When
the product line standby and programmed expenses were brought
under control, the loss in this line was curtailed, and profitability
improved. It was decided to retain the line, despite its low profit
contribution, because the company desired to retain its full-line
sales image. Pricing adjustments were made to adjust the low profit
contribution for this line.

ISOLATE AND EXPLODE

The ideas revealed in these exhibits have been termed concepts
of "isolate" and "explode," and are demonstrated in Exhibit 28.
From the corporate product line statement, the industrial product
line's performance can be "isolated" and the detail "exploded"
into a product line statement for the industrial group. This isolate
and explode concept, while valuable as a product line analysis tool,
will prove even more valuable when the expenses and revenues of
the sales divisions are analyzed.

THE ROLE OF STANDARDS IN REVENUE AND COSTS

The Badger Light Company is on a standard cost system. A
standard cost is a predetermined cost. It is a concept that dates
to the scientific management work of Frederick W. Taylor, one
of the first management consultants, and is generally associated
with job costing within a company. At Badger Light the benefits
of standard costing can be illustrated. When merchandise is turned
over to the marketing group at standard cost (as in Exhibit 6),

ISOLATE AND EXPLODE

CORPORATE STATEMENT					
	Total Company	Product Lines			
		Residen-tial	Archi-tectural	Indus-trial	
Gross sales	$27,240	$4,560	$18,398	$4,282	
Variable costs	17,338	2,630	10,848	3,860	
Profit contribution	9,902	1,930	7,550	422	
Profit contribution percentage	36.3	42.2	41.0	9.8	
Specific product expenses	2,090	1,028	800	262	
Product earnings	7,812	902	6,750	160	
General expenses	6,002				
Earnings before taxes	1,810				

ISOLATE

STATEMENT OF EARNINGS—RESIDENTIAL

STATEMENT OF EARNINGS—ARCHITECTURAL

STATEMENT OF EARNINGS—INDUSTRIAL			
	Total Industrial	Product Line	
		Fluorescent	Street Lights
Gross sales	$4,282	$2,444	$1,838
Variable costs	3,860	2,083	1,777
Profit contribution	422	361	61
Profit contribution percentage	9.8	14.8	3.3
Specific product line expenses	204	105	99
Product line earnings	218	256	(38)
Product line earnings—index	0.52	0.71	(0.62)
General product line expenses	58		
Industrial product group earnings	160		

EXPLODE

Exhibit 28

four key variables, price, volume, mix, and the expense budget, can be isolated as the responsibilities of the marketing group.

The price variance measures one of these three possible deviations from the sales plan. It is an expression of variation from planned profit. When sales forecasts are combined with standard variable costs expressed in the profit plan, the effect of actual variations from the planned volume, the planned mix of sales, and planned prices can be measured separately in terms of a gain or loss in standard profit contribution. The price variance is computed from the difference between actual sales at actual prices and actual sales at standard prices. Actual sales at standard price less standard variable costs are used to compute the actual standard profit contribution for the reporting period. The difference between this amount and the planned amount of standard profit contribution is explained by volume and mix variances.

The volume variance is the difference between actual sales and planned sales, multiplied by the planned percentage of standard profit contribution.

The mix variance is the difference between the actual percentage of profit contribution received and the planned percentage of standard profit contribution, multiplied by the actual sales volume at standard prices. This variance is the result of selling a different mix than planned of the products within a product line that has varying standard profit contribution per item. These calculations are performed separately for each product line. This is done where there is considerable variation in the rate of profit contribution among the different products within a product line. In some cases where there is little variation within product lines, the company may prefer to report the mix variance between product lines as a gross figure rather than computing these figures for the individual products.

Some companies do not maintain standard selling prices (list prices), but simply use sales at actual prices to compute a volume and mix variance from planned profit contribution. The effect is that any price variance is combined into the mix and volume variances reported.

The absolute correctness of one particular method of calculating these variances is not as important as the advantage of reporting such data, even if based on rather crude calculations. Variances focus attention on the individual elements which make up total planned sales, and permit variations from plan to be measured in terms of their effect on profit.

In the Badger Light Company, as shown in Exhibit 29, the marketing variances are identified. The statement of planned earnings vs. actual earnings was prepared for the executive vice president's examination. Since he wanted a further breakdown of the sales variances by product line, the variance analysis shown in Exhibit 30 was prepared; the price, volume, and mix variances by product line are illustrated. The other responsibility variances are shown on this report, so performance variances can be traced to the

STATEMENT OF EARNINGS, PLANNED VS. ACTUAL
The Badger Light Company
Year Ended December 31, 1968
(000's omitted)

	Plan	Actual	Variance
Gross	$26,878	$27,240	$ 362
Standard variable costs	17,177	17,400	(223)
Standard profit contribution	9,701	9,840	139
Standard profit contribution percentage	36.12%	36.09%	
Specific product expenses	2,012	2,090	(78)
Product earnings	7,689	7,750	
General expenses	5,866	5,940	(74)
Earnings before taxes	$ 1,823	$ 1,810	$ (13)

Summary of variances

Sales variances		$ 139
Price	.2	
Volume	130.6	
Mix	(8.2)	
Performance variances		(152)
Net total		$ (13)

Exhibit 29

Variance Analysis
The Badger Light Company
(000's omitted)

Sales variances by product line

	Total	Product Line A	Product Line B	Product Line C
Price	$ 0.2	$ 4.3	$ 1.4	$(5.5)
Volume	130.6	42.3	26.2	62.1
Mix	8.2	38.8	(23.4)	(7.2)
	$139	$85.4	$ 4.2	$49.4

Cost variances by responsibility

Factory X	$ (99)
Factory Y	(114)
Factory Z	46
Personnel	2
Finance	6
Product styling	3
Warehousing	—
Tooling	41
Merchandising	(6)
Corporate	(13)
Selling	(18)
	$(152)

Exhibit 30

responsibility center requiring attention. (Also see Exhibits 31, 32, and 33.)

The executive vice president understands that "true cost" does not exist. However, in the portrayal of cost for a particular product line or function, it is essential to strip away allocations

ADDITIONAL DETAIL OF SELLING EXPENSES BY
VARIABLE, SPECIFIC, AND GENERAL CATEGORIES
The Badger Light Company
Year Ended December 31, 1968
(000's omitted)

	Variable	Specific	General
Salaries			
Salesmen's compensation			
Commissions	$1,461	$1,461	
Prizes and awards	190	$ 35	$ 155
Sales and merchandising			
District sales managers	386		386
Merchandising managers	102	102	
Styling managers	137	114	23
Advertising	72	58	14
Sales offices	243		243
Drafting	76	43	33
Contract	143	101	42
Advertising and promotion			
Advertising			
Consumer publications	360	360	
Trade, professional, industrial			
publications	194	194	
Catalogs and price lists	214	214	
Direct mail circulars	75	75	
Displays	35	35	
Promotion			
Shows	39	27	12
Distributor training	51		51
Salesmen's samples	36	36	
Other selling expenses			
Sales offices	210		210
Sales discounts	195	195	
Markdowns on finished goods	430	430	
Travel and entertainment	106	34	72
Cost of returns	152	152	
Shipping expenses			
Wages and salaries	475	308	167
Rentals and depreciation	211		211
Supplies and maintenance	196	140	56
Total	$5,789	$2,104 $2,010	$1,675

Exhibit 31

DETAIL OF GENERAL AND ADMINISTRATIVE EXPENSES BY
VARIABLE, SPECIFIC, AND GENERAL CATEGORIES
The Badger Light Company
Year Ended December 31, 1968
(000's omitted)

	Variable	Specific	General
Salaries			
Executive staff	$ 490		$ 490
Controller's staff	64		64
Systems group	84		84
Credit and accounts receivable	91	$ 27	64
Data processing	135		135
Billing supervisor and clerks	32	12	20
Order control and processing	31	10	21
Phone operators and office boys	21		21
Other expenses			
Postage	46		46
Stationery and supplies	125	56	69
Telephone and telegraph	37		37
Credit rating bureau	9		9
Trade associations	11	$ 5	6
Rental of data processing equipment	183		183
Repairs	13		13
Travel expense	47	21	25
Professional fees	164	27	137
Insurance	14		14
State and local taxes	65		65
Contributions	51		51
Provision for doubtful accounts	96	27	69
Depreciation	9		9
	$1,818	$105	$80	$1,633

Exhibit 32

and isolate the attributable cost factors. The isolation of these costs allows management to concentrate on factors that are subject to the management decision processes.

Once the analysis of product group earnings was completed, the executive vice president and the sales manager directed their attention to the sales organization and the other areas of marketing effort, the channels of distribution, and the performance regarding individual customers. The next analysis that was requested was profitability by market segments, and profitability by sales area.

STATEMENT OF PLANNED EARNINGS
The Badger Light Company
Year Ended December 31, 1968
(000's omitted)

Gross sales	$26,878
Standard variable costs	17,177
Standard profit contribution	9,701
Standard profit contribution percentage	36.1%
Specific product expenses	2,012
Planned product earnings	7,689
General expenses	5,866
Planned earnings before taxes	$ 1,823

Exhibit 33

Chapter V

Market Segment Profitability

THE ANALYSIS of marketing activities discussed thus far has been from a product manager's point of view as expressed to the executive vice president of a typical company. In many companies the only detailed breakout of cost and revenue information is in the form of product line statements similar to those shown in Exhibit 16.

The product line "cut" is most common because cost and revenue information are normally assembled by product line, and businessmen most often look at their businesses as a series of product lines or product-oriented centers. This is only one of the "functional" areas of possible cost information, or "cuts."

There are four functional areas to which marketing costs can be assigned, and they reflect the four functional areas of marketing:

1. Product lines.
2. Responsibility centers (division, district, territory).
3. Channel of distribution (wholesale, direct).
4. Customers.

Profitability analysis is appropriate and should be available for each of these areas; cost and revenue figures must be transferable or "sortable" among the areas. This is the underlying assumption behind the "building block" concept. The specific-general cost switches that occur for an expense when the cut changes among areas will change the level of acceptable profitability when the area under observation changes. A nationwide 30 percent product line contribution may be acceptable, but the goal for a wholesale channel of distribution may be 40 percent, and a sales territory may require a 60 percent contribution to be considered acceptably profitable.

To demonstrate how cost and revenue figures can be sorted into several functional areas, we will examine the type of information available to the field sales manager at our sample firm, the Badger Light Company.

The field sales manager has been asked to evaluate channels of distribution and sales division performance. Using the company's information system, he has started to isolate and explode information in order to track pockets of opportunity and poor performance.

REVIEW OF COST CHARACTERISTICS

A specific or general cost is meaningful only in relation to the object of measurement under consideration. The object of profit measurement may change if a cost is specific or general. For example, the merchandise manager's salary at Badger Light Company is specific to the product line; it is solely and directly related to and associated with his products. This would apply to a brand manager's salary as well. However, when these merchandise or brand managers' salaries are considered in the cost of the sales division's operations, they are general costs, not associated with any one district. On the other hand, the division sales manager's salary is a general cost when the costs associated with product management are considered; but it is a specific cost, applicable to the division he manages, when the division is the object of measurement.

Some costs are specific regardless of the object of measurement; others, such as corporate office expense, cannot be identified with products or divisions and are general costs in both categories. In some cases, a given expense may even be partially specific and partially general in relation to the object of measurement under consideration.

An example of this is a company that advertises a specific product or brand and the corporate name in separate advertising programs. When assessing product earnings, the expense category "advertising" will be partially specific and partially general. This is illustrated in Exhibit 34. While the gross sales of $27,000,000 of Badger Light and the profit of $1,810,000 before taxes remain unchanged, other costs have shifted between the specific and general categories as the object of measurement has shifted from the product group to the sales division.

You will note in Exhibit 34 that the gross sales, variable costs, and profit contributions are the same for the two categories. Of general product group expense, $304,000 more of expense is specific to the sales divisions, and changes when the object of measurement changes from product group to sales divisions. This shift is shown with greater detail in Exhibit 35. In both exhibits the wholesale and contract channel of distribution cut within the sales division structure is discernible.

Both of these divisions are analyzed in the same manner as the product line. The variable costs are deducted from gross sales to arrive at a profit contribution. The specific sales division expenses are assigned to the respective divisions. The general sales division expenses, which include standby and programmed expenses, are not allocated between the two divisions.

In order to portray just those expenses that have shifted with the change of the object of measurement from product groups to the sales business, the field sales manager had a schedule constructed (Exhibit 36). This exhibit demonstrates how the specific selling expenses were split when the object of measurement changed.

EARNINGS STATEMENT
The Badger Light Company
Year Ended December 31, 1968
(000's omitted)

Product Group

	Total Company
Gross sales	$27,240
Variable costs	17,338
Profit contribution	9,902
Profit contribution percentage	36.3 %
Specific product group expenses	2,090
Product group earnings	7,812
Product group earnings index	0.79
General product group expenses	6,002
Earnings before taxes	$ 1,810

Sales Divisions

	Total Company	Wholesale	Contract
Gross sales	$27,240	$20,229	$ 7,011
Variable costs	17,338	12,664	4,674
Profit contribution	9,902	7,565	2,337
Profit contribution percentage	36.3 %	37.5 %	33.3 %
Specific sales division expenses	2,394	2,049	345
Sales division earnings	7,508	5,516	1,992
Sales division earnings index	0.76	0.73	0.85
General sales division expenses	5,698		
Earnings before taxes	$ 1,810		

Exhibit 34

EARNINGS STATEMENT
The Badger Light Company
Year Ended December 31, 1968
(000's omitted)

	Product Group	Sales Divisions		
	Total Company	*Total Company*	*Wholesale Division*	*Contract Division*
Gross sales	$27,240	$27,240	$20,229	$7,011
Variable costs				
Specific sales deductions				
Cash discounts allowed	195	195	195	—
Commissions	1,461	1,461	1,461	—
Trade discounts	210	210	210	—
Direct materials	11,909	11,909	3,166	3,743
Direct labor	1,870	1,870	1,357	513
Variable manufacturing overhead	1,140	1,140	835	305
Variable selling expenses	448	448	352	95
Variable administrative expenses	105	105	88	17
Profit contribution	9,902	9,902	7,565	2,337
Profit contribution percentage	36.3%	36.3%	37.5%	33.3%

Specific product group expenses (Total Company)

	Total Company
Selling—compensation	
Prizes and awards	35
Merchandising managers	102
Styling managers	114
Advertising department	58
Drafting	43
Contract	101

Specific divisions expenses

	Total Company	*Wholesale Division*	*Contract Division*
Selling—compensation			
Prizes and awards	190	190	—
District sales managers	386	386	—
Advertising department	2	—	2
Sales offices	243	243	—
Drafting	76	—	76
Contract	143	—	143

Selling—advertising and promotion	
Consumer publications	360
Trade, professional, and industrial publications	
Catalogs and price lists	214
Direct mail circulars	75
Displays	35
Shows	27
Salesmen's samples	36
Selling—other	
Markdowns	430
Travel and entertainment	34
Cost of returns	152
Administrative	
Professional fees	27
Trade associations	5
Bad debts	27
Travel expense	21
Product group earnings	7,812
Product group earnings—index	0.79
General expenses	
Selling	1,675
Administrative	1,633
Fixed manufacturing	2,694
Earnings before taxes	$ 1,810

Selling—advertising and promotion			
Consumer publications	360	360	—
Trade, professional, and industrial publications	18	—	15
Catalogs and price lists	209	161	48
Direct mail circulars	75	58	17
Displays	35	19	16
Shows	5	5	—
Distributor training	51	51	—
Salesmen's samples	36	34	2
Selling—other			
Sales offices	210	210	—
Travel and entertainment	106	98	8
Cost of returns	152	140	12
Administrative			
Bad debts	96	93	3
Division earnings	7,508	$ 5,516	$1,932
Division earnings—index	0.74	0.73	0.98
General expenses			
Selling	1,307		
Administrative	1,617		
Fixed manufacturing	2,694		
Earnings before taxes	$ 1,810		

Exhibit 35

OBJECT OF MEASUREMENT CHANGE IN
SPECIFIC SELLING EXPENSES
The Badger Light Company
Year Ended December 31, 1968
(000's omitted)

Product Groups		*Sales Divisions*
	Selling—compensation	
$ 155	Prizes and awards	$ —
386	District sales managers	—
—	Merchandising managers	102
23	Styling managers	137
14	Advertising department	70
243	Sales office	—
33	Drafting	—
42	Contract	—
	Selling—advertising and promotion	
	Trade, professional, and industrial	
—	publications	176
—	Catalogs and price lists	5
12	Shows	33
51	Distributor training	—
434	Shipping expenses	434
	Selling—other	
210	Sales offices	—
—	Markdowns	430
72	Travel and entertainment	—
$1,675		$1,387

Exhibit 36

DISTRICT AND TERRITORY EARNINGS

There are eight districts within the wholesale division of Badger Light Company. The profitability comparison of these districts is made in Exhibit 37. The district earnings may be contrasted as follows:

District	Profit Contribution Percentage	District Earnings per Dollar of 1968 Profit Contribution	District Earnings as a Percentage of 1968 Sales
Middle Atlantic	37.6	0.88	33.1
New England	37.9	0.87	33.0
West	37.8	0.85	32.1
Midwest	37.2	0.84	31.2
South	37.8	0.77	29.1
New York City	37.0	0.67	24.8
Chicago	35.6	0.68	24.2
Southwest	36.1	(0.27)	(9.8)

Examination of district earnings identifies two areas for further investigation:

1. The lower district earnings per dollar of profit contribution experienced in New York and Chicago.
2. The specific costs identified with Southwest district operations exceed the district profit contribution generated by sales.

Comparing these three districts with other districts, travel and entertainment expense, the cost of returns attributable to sales, and bad debts appear exceptionally high and suggest that an analysis of contribution by salesman is needed. The isolate and explode principle, isolating one district that concerns us, and exploding the facts necessary to complete an investigation out of our information bank, allows us to get more detail about the Southwest district.

STATEMENT OF TERRITORIAL EARNINGS, WHOLESALE DIVISION
The Badger Light Company
Year Ended December 31, 1968
(000's omitted)

	Total Wholesale	Districts							
		New England	Metro-politan New York City	Middle Atlantic	South	Metro-politan Chicago	Midwest	Southwest	West
Gross sales	$20,229	$2,436	$1,407	$4,213	$2,646	$1,417	$2,946	$ 643	$4,521
Profit contribution	7,565	922	520	1,583	1,000	504	1,097	232	1,707
Profit contribution percentage	37.5%	37.9%	37.0%	37.6%	37.8%	35.6%	37.2%	36.1%	37.8%
Specific district expenses	1,606	124	170	192	231	163	171	295	260
District earnings	5,959	$ 798	$ 350	$1,391	$ 769	$ 341	$ 926	$ (63)	$1,447
District earnings—index	0.79	0.87	0.67	0.88	0.77	0.68	0.84	(0.27)	0.85
General district expenses	443								
Wholesale division earnings	$ 5,516								

Exhibit 37

Detail for Exhibit 37

STATEMENT OF TERRITORIAL EARNINGS, WHOLESALE DIVISION

The Badger Light Company

Year Ended December 31, 1968

(000's omitted)

	Total Wholesale	New England	Metropolitan New York City	Atlantic	South	Metropolitan Chicago	Midwest	Southwest	West
						Districts			
Gross sales	$20,229	$2,436	$1,407	$4,213	$2,646	$1,417	$2,946	$ 643	$4,521
Profit contribution	7,565	922	520	1,583	1,000	504	097	232	1,707
Profit contribution percentage	37.5%	37.9%	37.0%	37.6%	37.8%	35.6%	37.2%	36.1%	37.8%
Specific district expenses									
Selling compensation									
Prizes and awards	190	15	—	70	47	—	—	3	55
District sales managers	386	44	51	42	41	53	54	47	54
Sales offices—salaries	243	16	25	17	48	30	35	43	29
Selling—advertising and promotion									
Catalogs and price lists	161	10	23	20	31	8	14	31	24
Direct mail circulars	58	4	12	7	3	14	4	3	11
Displays	19	—	4	—	3	7	2	—	3
Distributor training	51	4	6	3	6	8	7	4	11
Salesmen's samples	54	4	6	3	7	2	3	3	6

Exhibit 38 (continued on page 92)

Detail for Exhibit 37 (Continued)

	Total Wholesale	New England	Metropolitan New York City	Atlantic	South	Metropolitan Chicago	Midwest	Southwest	West
							Districts		
Selling and other									
Sales offices—other expenses	210	17	28	15	28	24	28	27	43
Travel and entertainment	98	4	4	10	14	11	12	32	11
Cost of returns	63	4	4	2	3	—	—	47	3
Administrative									
Bad debts	93	2	3	3	—	6	12	55	10
District earnings	5,959	$ 798	$ 350	$1,391	$ 769	$ 341	$ 925	$ (63)	$1,477
District earnings—index	0.79	0.87	0.67	0.88	0.77	0.68	0.94	(0.27)	0.85

General division expenses	
Selling	
Consumer publications	360
Shows	6
Cost of returns	77
Wholesale division earnings	$ 5,516

Exhibit 38

Since this district was the only one with a loss, it is the next district to be isolated and exploded for the executive vice president and the sales manager. This district's performance is shown in Exhibit 39. One salesman within the district, W. Lippincott, has the lowest sales volume, the lowest profit contribution, and the highest specific salesman expenses. Salesman performance may be summarized as follows:

Salesman	Profit Contribution Percentage	Salesman Earnings per Dollar of 1968 Profit Contribution	Salesman Earnings as a Percentage of 1968 Sales
R. F. Burr	39.1	0.60	23.4
A. Appleyard	36.9	0.82	30.2
W. Lippincott	24.6	(1.57)	(38.6)

STATEMENT OF CONTRIBUTION BY SALESMAN
Southwest District
The Badger Light Company
Year Ended December 31, 1968
(000's omitted)

	Total District	Territory Salesmen		
		R. F. Burr	A. Appleyard	W. Lippincott
Gross sales	$643	$361	$168	$114
Profit contribution	232	142	62	28
Profit contribution percentage	36.0	39.1	36.9	24.6
Specific salesman expenses	140	57	11	72
Salesman contribution	92	$ 85	$ 51	$(44)
Salesman contribution—index	0.40	0.60	0.82	(1.57)
General salesman expenses	155			
Southwest district loss	$(63)			

Exhibit 39

Examination of the other salesmen's performances indicates that there are three necessary areas of further inquiry:

1. Cost of returns. As indicated in Exhibit 40 in the category
    pertaining to cost of returns attributable to salesmen,
    the performances of Burr and Lippincott appear to be
    out of line.
2. Bad debt losses. Again Burr and Lippincott seem to be
    the problem.
3. Expenses. Salesmen's expenses, specifically attributable
    to Lippincott, exceed his profit contribution.

Since Lippincott has poor performance in all three categories
and his profit contribution is extremely low, the isolate and explode
technique singles out his territory. His activity by customer group
record is exploded from the data bank, as shown in Exhibit 41.

This analysis of Lippincott's activity reveals that most of his
sales are to small manufacturers. He has been emphasizing a mix
of products with the lowest profit contribution and, since he is
dealing with small manufacturers, his cost of returns and bad
debts is relatively high.

A further cut at Lippincott's territory could be made. This
would be product sales within customer group. If we were to display this cut, we would isolate small manufacturers and explode
the product mix sold to them. However, we have identified a
situation at the "grass-roots" level that indicates that one salesman
in a territory is emphasizing a poor product mix to customers of
dubious quality. This illustrates the value of the information
system. Management can control the profit structure when it has
the information to find the Lippincotts within the sales force and
align their performances with management goals.

There are two other market segments that the executive vice
president and marketing manager of the Badger Light Company
can analyze. They can conduct further comparative analysis
between the wholesale and contract channels of distribution, carrying this analysis down to the product-within-customer level.
They can also start with an analysis ranking customers by profit
contribution to determine where marketing emphasis is most
profitable, and determining what customers are not profitable
to maintain with full salesman contact.

The systems used in this analysis include a marginal income
approach. With this type of analysis "what if" questions can be

STATEMENT OF CONTRIBUTION BY SALESMAN
Southwest District
The Badger Light Company
Year Ended December 31, 1968
(000's omitted)

		Territory Salesmen		
	Total District	*R. F. Burr*	*A. Appleyard*	*W. Lippincott*
Gross sales	$643	$361	$168	$114
Profit contribution	232	142	62	28
Profit contribution percentage	36.0%	39.1%	36.9%	24.6%
Specific salesman expenses				
Selling				
Prizes and awards	3	2	1	—
Salesmen's samples	3	1	1	1
Travel and entertainment	32	14	6	12
Cost of returns	47	20	—	27
Administrative				
Bad debts	55	20	3	32
Salesmen's contribution	92	$ 85	$ 51	$(44)
Salesmen's contribution—index	0.40	0.60	0.82	(1.57)
General Salesmen's expenses				
Selling—compensation				
District sales manager	47			
Sales office	43			
Selling—advertising and promotion				
Catalogs and price lists	31			
Direct mail circulars	3			
Distributor training	4			
Selling—other				
Sales office expenses	27			
Southwest district loss	$(63)			

Exhibit 40

STATEMENT OF CONTRIBUTION BY W. LIPPINCOTT, BY CUSTOMER GROUP
The Badger Light Company
Year Ended December 31, 1968
(000's omitted)

	Total W. Lippincott	Small Manu-facturers	School Con-struction	Recrea-tional Night Lighting
		Customer Group		
Gross sales	$114	$85	$14	$15
Profit contribution	28	16	6	6
Profit contribution percentage	24.6%	18.9%	43.0%	40.0%
Specific customer group expense				
Selling				
Travel and entertainment	10	7	1	2
Cost of returns	27	18	4	5
Administration				
Bad debts	32	30	—	2
Customer group earnings	(41)	$(39)	$ 1	$ (3)
General customer group expenses				
Selling				
Salesman samples	1			
Travel and entertainment	2			
Salesman contribution	$(44)			

Exhibit 41

asked, and information can be used in other types of profitability analysis such as pricing, selective selling, or determinations of return on investment. Utilizing these types of analysis, the accounting system becomes a management decision tool rather than one for meeting the firm's custodial reporting requirements to shareholders and third parties such as the IRS.

SELECTIVE SELLING BASED ON PROFIT CONTRIBUTION

Since profit contribution analysis directs attention to the relative profitability of different products, it can be used as a guide for allocating selling effort to products selectively, with greater emphasis assigned to the products with higher rates of profit contribution. Advertising and sales promotion efforts can be focused on the most profitable products, or salesmen's compensation can be related to the profitability of their sales rather than to sales volume alone.

For example, a tool and die manufacturer distributed products through regional manufacturers' representatives who traditionally earned a commission of 10 percent on sales. These representatives also sold products of other, noncompeting manufacturers, and most of these sales yielded a 12 percent commission. Other representatives were getting a 12 percent commission from competitive tool and dye producers. An analysis of the company's original sales indicated that they were unduly concentrated in items with low profit contribution.

Based upon a profitability analysis, the firm's original commission structure was revised as follows: The company's products were grouped into a number of categories based upon their rate of profit contribution. Sales quotas were set in each category, and the commissions rate remained at 10 percent for sales up to these quotas. On additional sales above the quotas, the commission ranged from 12 percent in the category with the lowest rate of profit contribution to 20 percent in the category with the highest. The quotas were set higher in the categories with lower profit contribution. The commissions were set higher for the categories with higher profit contribution.

The revised commission structure was received favorably by the representatives, and within a few months a marked improvement occurred in the overall rate of the company's profit contribution. Some representatives who had never before sold any of the items in the category of highest profit contribution were selling significant amounts within three months.

In this case and in similar cases with other firms, acceptance by sales personnel of a sales incentive plan geared to profit contribution was gained by assuring that the new plan did not reduce commissions for the existing volume and mix of sales. A method of assuring this is outlined in Exhibit 42. In this situation, a compensation rate was established after the base of profit contribution was attained in the sales territory, and additional sales incentive

Evaluation Technique—Incentive Program

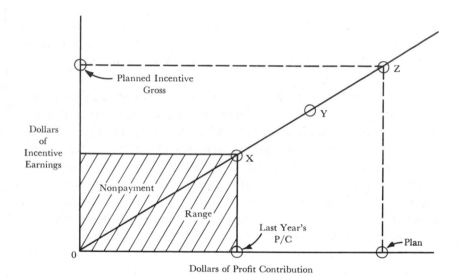

No incentive paid   O–X

Rate to be paid   X–Z

Payment at specific P/C   Y

Exhibit 42

compensation was computed on sales above the base quota. The salesmen's normal concern that the new compensation program would cut into their former earnings was the reason for limiting the changes in commission rates to sales in excess of quota. Commissions were held at previous levels, and incentive bonuses were used to direct effort. More importantly, their concern reflects a realistic appreciation of the probable effect of a selective selling structure. It will probably change the sales mix without necessarily increasing the sales volume. In this case, the tool and die manufacturer was able to increase sales by increasing the effort his nonexclusive agent salesmen extended on selling the firm's products. It is important that the commission and incentive structure be designed so that both the company and the sales people benefit from the change in mix.

In the Badger Light Company, a commission structure problem was also identified. The significance of this will be covered when we discuss territory performance.

Chapter VI

Programmed Costs

PROGRAMMED COSTS are planned costs which will be incurred because of a specific management policy decision. Typically, a given commitment to programmed costs can be altered by a countermanding management decision. This is often necessary when there is a change in business conditions or in competition. Some examples of marketing programmed costs are advertising costs, some research and development costs, and sales promotion expense. The profit effect of a programmed cost may not be realized in the year of decision or in the year of expenditure.

There are three basic elements which explain the nature and problems inherent in the programmed cost area: planning, timing, and policy. A programmed cost is a policy cost responsive to a plan. It is a part of the management policy or decision area and, therefore, is responsive to planning. These costs have been called discretionary or managed costs to indicate that management decides their "right" amount in any year or other time period.

Attempts are being made through modern management techniques to optimize the relationship of revenue to programmed costs. Some of these methods involve the opportunity cost rate concept, which relates sales results to expenditures. This concept will be discussed in this chapter. The emphasis on management information systems and the appropriateness, timing, and quality of information are indications of some of the efforts to find and control the revenue-cost relationship in this area. Often the development of some information, where there is little or no intention, and some indication of cost/revenue relationships are beneficial to provide more of a "feel" than the "feel" that management may currently have.

It is difficult to portray the timing of the cost versus revenue matrix in an accounting system tied to a yearly report. Typically, programmed costs are incurred long before the sales effects of the cost are realized. In an accounting (custodial) sense, it is normal to charge the programmed expense to the time period in which it is incurred. However, the full effect on sales and earnings may be months or even years from the date of expense. Further, there is no assurance that an incremental expenditure for advertising or promotion will mean proportionately higher sales. Sales may increase more rapidly at low levels of advertising expenditure than at high levels, because of product life or distribution differences. Also, there may be a carry-over effect; and the impact of expenditures made now may take place some time in the future rather than immediately. This is similar to a decay effect, whereby customer loyalty built by past promotions or satisfaction tends to decay slowly in the absence of further promotion. Other areas that affect timing are the environment, competitive reaction, product quality, promotion, and human reaction.

Regardless of the frustrations in precisely predicting the result of a given programmed expense, it is still necessary to maintain control of these expenses and to develop means to measure their effect. The magnitude of most programmed expense, such as advertising expenditures, makes it necessary to exercise this control.

Programmed marketing costs are focused on individuals and groups outside the company. They generally are incurred to influence external behavior through communication such as advertising or promotion. Typically, they involve continued experimentation within product lines and within geographic areas to attempt to find the best increment of programmed costs.

Through experience, advertisers have evolved a concept of typical advertising effectiveness. This conceptual relationship of expenditure to sales is portrayed in Exhibit 43, which shows an increment of sales that would be in existence without advertising (point A), a point where incrementally little additional return is realized from additional low levels of advertising expenditure (point B), and another point where advertising expenditures tend to accelerate sales dramatically (point C). Later, the exhibit portrays a point where sales level off and the expenditure is not worthwhile. Point C on the exhibit is the theoretical optimum point of an advertising expenditure. It is this point toward which marketers are ideally striving in their experimentation. This optimum point, from the viewpoint within the company, is the combination of effective distribution, sales force employment, advertising efforts, promotional expenditures, and, of course, a viable product.

The effectiveness of the programmed marketing decision, or the lack of effectiveness, will have an impact on all of the functional and administrative groups within the company. With the magnitude of the advertising decision being what it is in a consumer goods company, the very profitability of a firm is in question when the advertising decision is made. An industrial company's overall activity will rely upon maintaining the orderly flow of sales or bookings to maintain the efficiency of the production force.

PROGRAMMED COSTS AND MARKETING DECISIONS

Measurement is difficult. The causes of human purchase behavior and the effects of behavioral patterns are difficult to project into marketing plans and specific strategies. In order to have enough experience upon which to base judgments, systematic information retention is necessary so trends can be projected and measures devised to quantify and apply marketing experience. Within the decision-making process, there are specific stages necessary to make the programmed cost decision. These stages include:

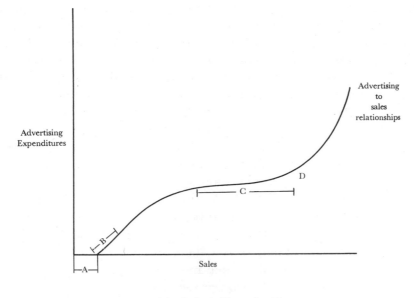

A = Sales obtained without advertising

B = Little additional return

C = Maximum advertising/sales cost efficiency

D = Optimum advertising cost/sales point

Exhibit 43

1. Identifying objectives and measures of attainment.
2. Stating alternative courses of action.
3. Estimating results.
4. Identifying interdependencies within the company and external environment.
5. Employing the feedback and control mechanism.

Measurement of objectives within the decision-making process includes the stating of objectives and alternates. This requires planning, not of subjective values, but of precise, quantified goals. In order to measure the programmed cost effect in advertising, the advertising objective must be stated in terms such as: "We want to increase our penetration of the market by 10 percent at a cost of one million dollars in national advertising." Penetration can be translated into dollar sales and profit contribution, to be compared with the additional advertising expenditure. The goals or objectives should not be stated in vague terms such as "We want to increase our penetration of the market," which does not define the acceptable result or the profit consequences of the decision.

When the objectives of marketing expenditures are stated and defined, the data required for measuring objectives can be specified. Nielsen or other external data to determine share of the market must now be collected, retained, and sorted. The cost of these data and their form and availability are important considerations. Often, information can be gathered by salesmen on calls. In any case, the organization of a program to obtain external data should be started. In order to prevent a "cart-before-the-horse" problem, the objectives to be achieved and measured must be specified before a data collection program is designated or purchased. To collect data or buy them and not know their end use adds to marketing costs and often results in additional numbers to confuse and clutter the decision process.

The data should identify the size and characteristics (demographic, financial) of the markets into which the product is being sold. The dimensions of potential markets should be defined, and the nature of customers and their consumption patterns specified. Potential competitive actions and reactions should also be identified and quantified.

Once data are gathered and diagnosed, the data bank for the company is formed. The "data bank" concept involves defining the smallest bits and pieces of information to be utilized in the firm's reporting and control process. Storage of this information and the ability to retrieve it for integration of external data with internal information is the function of the data bank. If the data are properly organized, they will be available for utilization in forecasting and reporting. These forecasts will form the assumptions upon which programmed expense decisions are made.

Adequate available data and management imagination, aggressiveness, and skill will produce the atmosphere for the stating of alternate courses of action. A good information system pays off when management can "game" and test hypothetical courses of action during their planning process. "Blue skying" or "buzz sessions," where ideas are freely exchanged, are valuable when the system permits quantification of the alternatives produced, and decisions are made on the basis of *pro forma* results.

DIFFERENTIAL COSTS AND REVENUES

As part of programmed cost planning, the notion of differential costs and revenues must also be considered. For example, in each promotion program the differential should be forecast between the profitability of the product line with a promotion and the volume and profit that would be realized if the promotion were not run. The alternative with the best profit differential is probably the best alternative.

Once alternatives have been quantified, a series of forecasts, or estimates of programmed costs and results, should be made. The detail of these projections depends upon the size and import-ance of the promotion. However, the promotion cost/results re-lationship should be projected by product and by market to assure awareness of the size and complexities of the cost decision. These types of estimates assist in defining the characteristics of data needed to control sales and marketing effort.

MONETARY BUDGETS

After the marketing appropriation is made, based upon the best information of the market available at the time of decision, the appropriation should be treated as a fixed budget. Actual ex-penses are then reported against the budget, and the budget becomes part of the marketing plan. If increments of promotion or marketing expense graph as a step-fixed expense as shown in Exhibit 44, this semivariable or semifixed expense pattern is altered when either additional sales volumes are reached or the marketing or economic conditions that defined the plan change.

In the programmed expense pattern shown in Exhibit 44, a toy manufacturer decided to spend $100,000 in spot TV ad-vertising for the first 50,000 units sold. He then decided to spend an additional $50,000 when his sales hit 50,000 units, and an

ADVERTISING APPROPRIATION—SEMIVARIABLE ALLOCATION

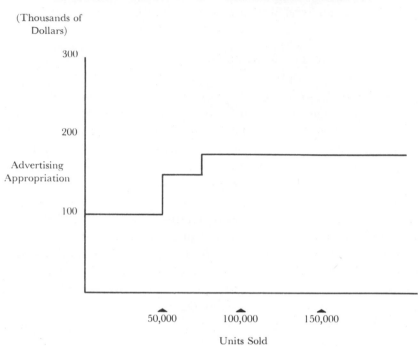

Exhibit 44

additional $12,500 when the sales were at 75,000 units. The plan described the management decision, and the advertising manager was able to proceed with the program.

THE ADVERTISING APPROPRIATION

Since advertising is generally the largest programmed marketing expense, the philosophies and assumptions underlying the appropriation are important.

The expectation that an outlay for advertising will result in some measure of profit contribution underlies any advertising appropriation. In theory, the optimum advertising appropriation is that point where the marginal cost, or incremental expenditure for one more unit of advertising, is equal to the marginal revenue or additional income from the sale of the additional units of product resulting from the advertising expenditure. This is nice in theory, but is almost impossible to define; it is necessary to develop other methods to aid judgment when making the appropriation.

There are basically three methods in use to establish the amount for an advertising appropriation. These are the incremental method; the percentage of sales method; and the objective and task method.

The incremental method assigns a unit cost of advertising to each unit sold or purchased. An example would be a two-dollar-per-unit initial expense assigned to the toys previously mentioned, or the assignment of twenty-five dollars advertising per car by an automobile manufacturer.

In the percentage of sales method, a percentage is assumed to be the allowable figure for advertising, and this percentage is committed as the appropriation, based upon the initial sales forecast. An example of this type of appropriation would be a 2 percent appropriation based on $500,000 of sales in a product line. This results in an appropriation of $10,000.

The incremental and percentage of sales methods treat advertising as a variable or semivariable sales cost. Additional expenditures of advertising are made on a per-unit increment assignment or on a percentage of total revenues.

The third method, the objective and task method, is the most common in American industry. In this concept, the objectives of an advertising program are outlined, and the cost to attain the objectives is computed and then budgeted.

The magnitude of advertising expenditures and their relationship to corporate profits are shown in Exhibit 45. In this exhibit, total annual U.S. advertising expenditures are compared with corporate net profits. In 1967, 17 billion dollars were spent for advertising, and approximately 39.3 billion dollars were reported as net profits by all U.S. corporations. By using the advertising expenditure and net profit figures, a ratio of advertising to net profit or an advertising earnings ratio is developed. Since 1960 there has been a ratio of approximately .45. This is a relationship of 45 cents of advertising being spent for each dollar of net profit. No one can claim this to be a causal relationship, and many will say it is far from a direct one. The fact that there is some relationship, however, gives marketers a tool to use as an aid to judgment.

ADVERTISING/EARNINGS RATIOS—ALL U. S. MANUFACTURING CORPORATIONS

	1950	1960	1961	1962	1963	1964	1965	1966	1967
Advertising (in billions) *	$ 5.8	$11.9	$12.0	$12.9	$13.5	$14.5	$15.6	$16.8	$17.3
Net Profits (in billions) †	20.9	24.4	23.3	26.6	28.8	32.7	38.7	43.1	39.3
Ratio of Advertising to Net Profits	.28	.49	.52	.48	.47	.44	.40	.39	.44

*From *Advertising Age.*
†From *Survey of Current Businesses.*

Exhibit 45

ADVERTISING/EARNINGS RATIOS PER DOLLAR—SELECTED CORPORATIONS

	1961	1963	1964	1965	1966	1967
General Motors	.16	.10	.10	.08	.12	.11
Eastman Kodak	.23	.28	.22	.17	.13	.14
Coca-Cola	.78	.85	.90	.85	.80	.72
Procter & Gamble	1.22	1.45	1.69	1.64	1.52	1.54
Jos. Schlitz Brewing	2.73	2.40	2.44	2.18	2.22	1.83
Pillsbury	3.72	3.34	3.38	2.15	2.47	2.31
Chrysler	4.26	.37	.37	.34	.44	.39
Miles Laboratories	5.02	4.47	4.25	4.04	4.28	4.24
Lever Bros.	8.29	6.45	5.82	5.90	12.30	8.60
Colgate-Palmolive	11.59	29.69	23.89	21.11	13.57	12.35
Alberto-Culver	16.46	10.15	9.55	—	9.51	6.12

In Thousands of Dollars

	1961	1963	1964	1965	1966	1967
Colgate-Palmolive						
Advertising	$57,000	$70,000	$82,000	$95,000	$95,000	$105,000
Earnings	4,919	2,358	3,432	4,500	7,000	8,500
Alberto-Culver						
Advertising	14,500	34,000	40,000	—	25,400	28,300
Earnings	881	3,351	4,186	—	2,672	4,624
Miles						
Advertising	27,500	28,000	29,500	33,000	36,500	38,500
Earnings	5,480	6,263	6,940	8,173	8,526	9,086

Exhibit 46

ADVERTISING, SALES PROMOTION, AND MARKETING OPPORTUNITY RATES
The Badger Light Company

Salesmen for District	Sales	Profit Contribution		Advertise. Expense	Advertise. Opportun. Rate	Sales Promotion Expense	Sales Promotion Opportun. Rate	Sales Expense	Sales Opportun. Rate	Total Marketing Expense	Marketing Opportun. Rate
		$	%								
R. F. Burr	$361	$142	39.1	$20	.14	$13	.09	$ 57	.40	$ 90	.62
A. Appleyard	$168	62	36.9	17	.27	7	.11	11	.18	35	.56
W. Lippincott	$114	28	24.6	14	.50	6	.21	72	2.56	92	3.28
District	$643	$232	36.0	$51	.22	$26	.11	$140	.50	$217	.93

Advertising Opportunity Rate → Advertising Expense Profit Contribution

Sales Promotion Opportunity Rate → Sales Promotion Profit Contribution

Sales Expense Opportunity Rate → Sales Expense Profit Contribution

Exhibit 47

The range of these advertising/earning ratios is shown in Exhibit 46, where a number of companies' ratios are shown. In industries where large advertising expenditures are common, such as the health and beauty aids group, the advertising/earnings ratio for companies within the industry is characteristically high, far over 1.00. Colgate-Palmolive in 1963 spent $29.70 for each $1.00 of net profit, and Alberto-Culver has spent between $9.59 and $16.50. Miles Laboratories has ranged fairly consistently in the $4.00 to $5.00 range. With advertising expenditures of this magnitude, overspending by an advertising manager can quickly spend a company out of profits, or a cutback in advertising can generate a rapid short-term cash flow.

The opportunity rate is a concept that has evolved from the ability to compare an expense with a profit contribution in ratio form. This concept, for use within a company to compare opportunity situations, investments, sales territories, and alternative uses of programmed expense, is illustrated in Exhibit 47. An advertising opportunity rate is derived by dividing an advertising expense by profit contribution; a sales promotion opportunity rate is the sales promotion dollars divided by profit contribution; and a sales expense opportunity rate is computed by dividing the sales expense by profit contribution.

The opportunity rate concept allows a manager to identify pockets of opportunity where the incremental application of advertising or effort can result in incrementally higher profit contributions. It also assists in identifying areas of overspending; and when set in a trend format, it allows the identification of areas where sales expense or other programmed costs tend to be less efficient than other available uses of marketing dollars. The utilization of this opportunity rate concept will be illustrated later for the Badger Light Company and in explaining the concept of the integrated marketing/financial information system.

Chapter VII

Sales Territory Analysis

At both the corporate management and field sales management levels, information is necessary to measure daily marketing performance. The problems encountered at the corporate level were discussed in previous chapters, when we looked at the problems of measuring marketing activity through the eyes of the executive vice president of the Badger Light Company.

At the sales territory or field selling levels, sales performance is a dynamic and daily problem. Through the process of territorial performance analysis, products and people are tested; and advertising and marketing efforts result in sales and profits. It is through the available sales territory analysis statistics that the crucial line supervision of salesmen occurs.

The supervision of salesmen selling a multiproduct line requires deft handling. This supervision must be based on more than emotion; it must be backed by timely information and accurate figures. In the past, sales managers have made sales calls and have supervised salesmen, with no better information than gross territorial dollar sales, and with no accurate knowledge of the mix of units sold within the product lines or of the mix of products sold to customers in the territory. The supervisory dialogue between the sales manager and the salesmen in these cases must be vague, often based upon the subjective judgments of the supervisor. In many ways, under these conditions, the supervisory process resembles a fighter trying to box his way out of a paper bag. No matter how he punches, the energy of the punch is absorbed in the bag; and he really doesn't know his effectiveness.

In order to be effective, sales management needs information, which is necessary for salesmen's supervision and evaluation, and for territorial comparison.

SALES AS AN INDICATOR

Sales, in dollars or units, are an obvious barometer of territory performance. Territories can be compared by using gross or net sales. Net sales can be defined as sales less returns, and net of price concessions. In companies with only one product line, gross and net sales are an effective means of comparison. However, in most multiproduct line companies, the use of just a sales figure for comparison or supervision can hide serious product mix or pricing problems. Also, the posting of a gross or net sales figure does not indicate whether the salesmen or sales territory is performing in accord with plans or potential.

Another means of territorial comparison besides sales, in units or dollars, must be used to obtain perspective. This comparison is obtained by the use of sales versus an indicator. The indicator can be a plan, a buying power index, or a PAR.

Planned sales indicators. These are comparisons of sales against a plan. The plan can be management's or the salesman's. The plan can be built up, from the sales territories, or generated down, from management. The use of a buying power index, such as *Sales Management* magazine's "BPI" or the Hearst Trading Area system of sales control, can be used as the comparative goal at three levels of operation. These levels of sales analysis are:

1. Nationwide.
2. A sectional or principal trading center.
3. Individual territories.

At each of these levels the Buying Power Index for the area or markets covered can be adjusted to portray the total area covered as 100 percent of potential. In Exhibit 48, an analysis of the Alabama trading areas is shown. Twelve consumer trading areas with 1.44 percent of the total Buying Power Index of the United States are equated to 100 percent, the total territory. Of company sales, $300,000 have been evaluated so they equal 100 percent.

These sales have then been compared with the Buying Power

ANALYSIS OF THE ALABAMA TRADING AREAS

Consumer Trading Area	Buying Power Index*	Territory at 100%	Your Company Sales	Sales at 100%	Index of Perform- ance
Anniston	.0520	3.59%	$ 10,000	3.33%	93
Birmingham	.4659	32.18	90,000	30.00	93
Decatur	.0507	3.50	6,000	2.00	57
Dothan	.0946	6.53	1,000	.33	5
Florence	.0671	4.64	20,000	6.67	144
Gadsden	.0903	6.24	29,000	9.67	154
Huntsville	.0793	5.48	32,000	10.67	195
Mobile	.2382	16.46	50,000	16.67	101
Montgomery	.1764	12.19	40,000	13.33	110
Opelika	.0199	1.37	3,000	1.00	73
Selma	.0443	3.06	9,000	3.00	98
Tuscaloosa	.0689	4.76	10,000	3.33	70
Total	1.4476	100.00%	$300,000	100.00%	

*From *The General Market Buying Power Index*, Hearst Publications.

Exhibit 48

Index to arrive at an "index of performance." In one trading area the company's sales performance rate is only 5 percent of the Buying Power Index, while in another trading area, Huntsville, an index of performance of 195 percent is being achieved. (In Huntsville the company's sales are 195 percent of what they would be if all territories performed exactly at the rate of the Buying Power Index.)

A Buying Power Index presumes that the territorial sales pattern of a company will follow the pattern of the indicator or the Buying Power Index. The Buying Power Index is a weighted index that shows a county's or market's proportionate share of national income, retail sales, factory payrolls, or other combinations of economic information. Once a good indicator is selected, one that adequately reflects the national distribution of sales for a company's products, management can develop skill in using the resultant index for analysis and forecasting of product and territory performance.

Should a company's sales not follow a Buying Power Index or predetermined pattern, PAR's can be set up for comparative purposes. A PAR is a composite of market research, industry statistics, and often judgment used to evaluate selling areas. It is tailor-made to evaluate a company's territorial sales and goals.

Sales by product line, within channel of distribution or by account classification, are other cuts of sales analysis. Since these penetrate the segments of marketing in great detail, the analysis must assume that a sales plan exists and that actual information is available to the level of detail being compared within the segment.

PROFIT CONTRIBUTION AS AN INDICATOR FOR TERRITORIAL PERFORMANCE

The best indicator for territorial control is a profit contribution target. With a report of profit contribution, the incremental effort of production or direct sales effort spent within the territory can be analyzed. The effort required to sell additional units of product can be isolated, and profitable sales areas can be examined and compared with other areas that are less profitable.

Territorial profit contribution can be compared against a standard profit contribution. When these exist, mix variances by territory can be computed by management at the field level; or corporate level management can see where volume, price, mix, and expense deviations exist. When these deviations are traced and become a means of sales force control, sophisticated reporting systems relying upon exception reporting can be used. And when these exist, management time can be saved in the control function and channeled into creative marketing.

Profit contribution figures give management the ability to trace where profitable operations exist. They allow management to identify unprofitable performance areas and to take action that clearly relate to "bottom-line profit."

OTHER COMPARISONS FOR TERRITORIAL ANALYSIS

There are numerous other bases available for comparing territories. Management can compare the number of salesman calls, the number of units sold, returns, expenses, pricing levels, service levels, order size level, lines written, unit size of sales, credit extended, shelf space, and market penetration. These comparisons, and many more, form a "shopping basket" of concepts which marketing management may utilize as standards of territorial measurement.

The list of comparisons among territories, whether they be sales, profit contribution, or the other comparison bases, merely forms the caption headings for the reports that management will select in its control process. Management, however, must realize that if it chooses to control by any one of these territorial indicators, it must then plan in terms of the same indicator at the same level of detail as the controls. Otherwise its control process will be meaningless.

THE PLANNING AND CONTROL LOOP

Planning and control has been described as a cyclical process, or a "planning loop." This loop starts with planning phases, passes through the concepts of control, and returns to the planning process through the feedback mechanism. This is illustrated in Exhibit 49.

In the planning phase the allocation of sales and marketing efforts is made. Reporting structures are also devised. Means must be available to evaluate territorial and market segment results. The cost and revenue "building blocks" must be able to be sorted into information that relates to corporate and marketing plans. Therefore, if advertising expenditures are made by area of country, the reporting system should display results and actual expenditures in terms of the planning areas. Market changes and statistical indicators showing demographic or geographic changes should also be related to the territorial or product reporting structure. This concept will be shown in the integrated marketing reporting system as "opportunity rate changes"; other statistical data are merged into the territorial reports which will be shown in a later chapter.

Exhibit 49

In the control process, sales and costs by product for territories must be reported. This is necessary to produce meaningful information on product mix and profitability, which will allow the rapid tracing of poor-quality sales performance. A poor quality of mix, producing disproportionately low profits in a large-volume district, must be identifiable if control is to be maintained.

Throughout the planning and control cycle, what is planned must be controlled. If there is a unit of planning, such as "call frequency by territory," there must also be a corresponding control reporting unit. If planning is performed but no subsequent report is generated, the planning becomes a meaningless exercise to be referred to at year-end and often wastefully re-created in an information vacuum.

Following is a series of report formats taken from companies using some of the territorial control concepts discussed. They present a variety of ideas and portray some of the numerous "cuts" that can be taken at basic sales district information.

The Territorial Report Structure

Territory Sales Statement (Exhibit 50). This report incorporates the basic trend statement for comparison of territories within a district. Planned sales are entered with an asterisk next to each figure at the beginning of the year. As each month's sales results are available, the actual sales figures are posted, and a variance from a planned figure is shown. Unfavorable variances are shown in parentheses.

In this type of statement, the number of data elements available in one report eliminates numerous subsidiary reports and provides a compact, concise territory or district sales tool. The following data elements are included:

1. Actual sales.
2. Planned sales.
3. Variances by month.
4. District totals of territories for all three elements.
5. Year-to-date figures for actual sales and variances.
6. A performance index.

Sales Territory Evaluation (Exhibit 51). This report is a printout by county for a territory. The information from the buying power index comparison presented earlier in this chapter is incorporated. An additional element of a Nielsen account column, indicating the number of chain stores and independent drugstores above $100,000 per year in sales, adds a dimension to the report that indicates the quality of accounts in the territory. Also, the distribution of actual accounts permits the computer to project the number of sales calls necessary for a level of coverage, based upon either the market potential or the company's current account makeup. These projected calls can be a tool for determining the size of sales territories and the workload of salesmen.

Territorial Statements—Channel of Distribution and Product Line Analysis (Exhibit 52). In this report the elements of gross sales, contribution percentage, returns, channel of distribution, product distribution of sales dollars, and a special indicator of "deal" percentage are displayed, comparing planned with actual results.

TERRITORIAL STATEMENTS
District 1
Sales
(in thousands of dollars)

1968	Territory 02		Territory 03		Territory 04		Territory 06		Territory 10		Territory 12		Total District 1	
	Var.	Actual Plan*	Var.	Actual Plan*	Var.	Actual Plan*	Var.	Actual Plan*	Var.	Actual Plan*	Var.	Actual Plan*	Var.	Actual Plan*
Jan.	1	25	0	22	(1)	10	(3)	16	1	20	0	27	(2)	120
Feb.	0	25	0	22	0	9	(2)	14	1	20	0	26	(1)	116
Mar.	1	20	0	22	0	9	(1)	14	1	17	0	25	1	107
Apr.	1	30	0	24	(1)	12	0	16	2	23	0	32	2	137
May		31*		26*		13*		16*		22*		32*		140*
Jun.		33*		28*		13*		17*		21*		33*		144*
Jul.		33*		30*		14*		17*		20*		37*		151*
Aug.		34*		32*		17*		17*		22*		38*		160*
Sep.		37*		34*		18*		18*		24*		37*		168*
Oct.		41*		39*		19*		18*		25*		41*		183*
Nov.		42*		41*		19*		19*		31*		46*		198*
Dec.		41*		37*		19*		18*		30*		43*		188*
Year to Date	3	100	0	90	(2)	40	(6)	60	5	80	0	110	0	480
Performance Index	3	101		78	(5)	94	(8)	75	7	117	0	98	0	93

Exhibit 50

SALES TERRITORY EVALUATION

County, State	Present Sales	Account Distribution				Nielsen			MSI Total Drug Sales	Projected Calls		Sales % Nat'l	BPI %	BPI $ Actual (Plan)	Plan Ed %	Quota Perf. %	Dollar Variance
		Drug	Chain	Drug Dept.	Whole-sale	Chain	Ind 100 199	Ind 200—		Nielsen	Meties						
Calhoun, Ala.	10,591	6	2	2	1	4	2	3	$790,500	76	108	.051	.04	10,500	.05	102.	91

Exhibit 51

TERRITORIAL STATEMENTS—CHANNEL OF DISTRIBUTION AND PRODUCT
LINE ANALYSIS
District 1
Cumulative Through April 1968

		Territory 02		Territory 03		Territory 04		Territory 06		Territory 10		Territory 12		Total District 1	
		Plan	Actual	Plan	Actual	Plan	Actual	Plan	Actual	Plan	Actual	Plan	Actual	Plan	Actual
														(in thousands of dollars)	
Sales $		103	100	90	90	38	40	54	60	85	80	110	110	480	480
Contribution	%	41.0	42.0	43.3	42.0	42.1	42.0	44.9	45.0	38.0	38.0	42.0	42.0	41.7	41.7
Return	%		2.4		2.5		2.5		2.6		2.5		2.5		2.5
Discount	%	20	20	20	19	18	18	18	20	28	28	16	18	20	20
Dept.	%	20	23	20	19	21	21	18	17	10	2	24	12	20	17
Chain	%	10	9	8	7	10	10	10	11	10	14	5	7	10	11
Total Direct	%	50	52	48	45	49	49	48	48	48	44	55	37	50	48
Wholesale	%	50	48	52	55	51	51	52	52	52	56	45	63	50	52
Hand Lotion	%														
Men's	%	100.0	100.0	100.0	100.0	100.0	100.0	100.0	100.0	100.0	100.0	100.0	100.0	100.0	100.0
Cosmetics	%														
Sets	%														
Teens	%														
Other	%														
Deal	%	47		49		56		67		38		45		51	

Exhibit 52

In this single report, we are able to see sales and contribution percentages and territorial relationships. The channel of distribution mix and the product mix by territory can be evaluated to determine whether our channel/product mix is satisfactory. In a consumer product situation where this report was used, a percentage of "deal" merchandise was essential to determine the impact of specific promotions and to maintain a level fill-in or regular stock reorders.

Key Account Report Exception Situations (Exhibit 53). This report, produced by territory, displays only those accounts where sales are more than 10 percent less than those of the preceding year. By just printing these exception situations within the territory, field management is alerted to lost accounts and to accounts where performance is significantly poorer than planned.

KEY ACCOUNT REPORT—EXCEPTION SITUATIONS

☒ Detail

☐ Summary   Territory No.   012

Account Number	Customer Name	This Month Sales	Year to Date Sales	Last Y T D Sales	Variance
07542	Jones Drugs	0	1,437	5,625	4,188
07070	Laurel Dept. Store	475	475	10,570	10,095
67423	Mountain Cut Rate Stores	42	5,240	8,570	3,330

Exhibit 53

Class of Trade Analysis for Salesmen's Territory—Matrix (Exhibit 54). By showing the classes of trade to which this company sells—independent drugstores, chain stores, supermarkets, department stores, wholesalers, and toiletry merchandisers—on one axis of a report; and by displaying the amount of product sold, by product line, into those classes of trade on the other axis, field management can see where "soft spots" exist within territories. Management also can see which product lines are showing strength in specific channels so emphasis can be applied and opportunities capitalized upon. By producing a penetration percentage by class of trade and by product, additional efforts within specific segments of the mar-

CLASS OF TRADE ANALYSIS FOR SALESMEN'S TERRITORY—MATRIX

Salesman: SLICK District: 1

Class of Trade	Reg./Deal.	Independ. Drug-stores	Chain Stores Drug	Variety	Disc.	Super-market	Dept. Stores Local	National	Whole-sale	T.M.	Deals. Units	Total for Month	Through Mo. 1 / Var	Total Year to Date Mo. 4 / Yr. 68	Var.	% Penet.
Hand Lotion	Reg.															
	Deal.															
Men's	Reg.		8,000	4,000	23,000		5,000	15,000	60,000			115,000	1,600	383,000	0	93
	Deal.															
Cosmetics	Reg.															
	Deal.															
Sets	Reg.															
	Deal.															
Teens	Reg.															
	Deal.															
Others	Reg.															
	Deal.															
Total by Month	Reg.		8,000	4,000	23,000		5,000	15,000	60,000			115,000	1,600	383,000	0	93
	Deal.															
Var.	Reg.		190	90	420			200	700				1,600			
	Deal.															
Total Year to Date	Reg.		27,000	13,000	78,000		14,000	50,000	201,000							
	Deal.															
Deals. Units	Reg.															
	Deal.															
Var. to Date	Reg.															
	Deal.															
% Penet.	Reg.		92	98	93		93	94	92							
	Deal.															

Exhibit 54

ket can be evaluted to see if they are worth further effort. This report allows management to identify "pockets of sales opportunity."

Customer Profitability Report (Exhibit 55). This report shows how the profit contribution concept can be used at the customer level. In the illustration, in the first quarter of the year this account had $55,000 less gross sales and $26,000 less profit contribution than planned. The account is also significantly behind the previous year's sales and profit contribution figures. These poorer-than-planned results occurred despite three more than planned sales calls being made, and the spending of twelve additional man-hours above the plan. In the promotional effort, $1,400 were spent on these sales calls.

CUSTOMER PROFITABILITY REPORT
First Quarter 1968
(in thousands of dollars)

Lyndon's Grocery Store
  Syracuse, New York
Profit Information

	1967	IQ 1968 Actual	IQ 1968 Planned
Gross sales	$100	$75	$130
Profit contribution	40	27	53

Sales Effort	No.	Man-Hours	Dollars
Planned calls	4	16	
Actual calls	7	28	1.4

Comments
  Customer emphasizing competitive brands due to alleged lack of cooperation with special promotions.

Action Planned

Exhibit 55

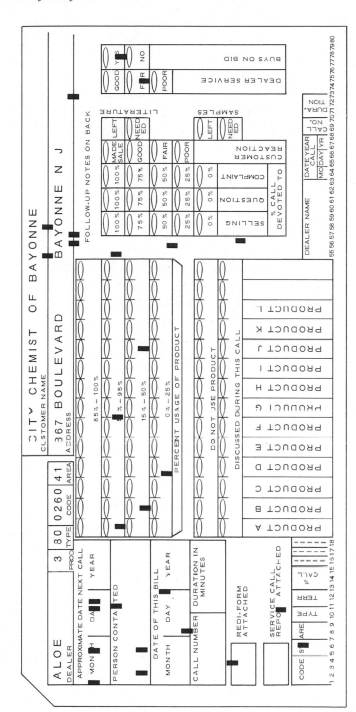

COMPUTERIZED JOURNEY REPORT—NEW CARD AS RETURNED FROM HOME OFFICE FOR NEXT CALL

Exhibit 56

In the "comments" section of Exhibit 55, the salesmen report the reasons for their poorer sales performance. The "action planned" space is left blank for management's description of a course of events to be planned for this account.

By producing this type of customer profitability report, particularly where single accounts are highly valued (in this case the actual profit contribution was $27,000 for this quarter), meaningful control can be obtained.

In order to pick up information for this type of profitability report, computerized journey reports such as the return card illustrated in Exhibit 55 can be used for salesmen's reporting.

Computerized Journey Report (Exhibit 56). This type of journey report or a conventional call report can be put into machine-readable form and entered into the data base, eventually to be merged into the territorial or account reporting process.

Other types of reports can be generated, such as *The Dealer Penetration Report* (Exhibit 57) and the *Report of Customer Reactions Termed "Poor"* (Exhibit 58), which are two special-situation reports that can be available from the data base.

Meaningful territorial reporting requires each company to tailor the reports produced to the needs and styles of its management. The reports must coincide with the level of planning and control it wants to develop. It is useless to produce a report if it is

DEALER PENETRATION REPORT
Product J
as of March 31, 1968

Percent Usage of Product

Region	0–15	15–50	50–85	85–100	Total Dealers
Eastern	4	17	38	4	63
Southern	31	2	4	5	42
Northern	27	14	2	4	47
Western	2	37	41	8	88
Total	64	70	85	21	240

Exhibit 57

REPORT OF CUSTOMER REACTIONS TERMED "POOR"
Week Ended March 31, 1968

Territory	*Customer*	*Product*
Eastern	Maywood Hospital, Pittsburgh, Pa.	K
	Kings Hospital, Newport, N.Y.	K
	Elbow Drug Co., Lyonsville, Md.	A, B, O, E
Western	San Jacinto State Hospital, Lee, Calif.	K
	California Public Health Service, Sacramento, Calif.	JK
Southern	Mobile Laboratories, Wheeling, Tex.	B

Exhibit 58

not meaningful, and if someone in the company is not going to use
the information to develop product or market plans and to control
performance. Unless the objectives of a report or reporting system
are defined in advance, the reporting system will become a pot-
pourri of data resulting neither in control of field sales forces nor
in the generation of sufficient information for effective sales analysis.

Chapter VIII

Special Analysis Situations

THE CONCEPTS of managerial accounting and direct costing are particularly useful where additional analysis is required to assure a full exploration of managerial alternatives. To illustrate one of these uses of decision-oriented analysis, the case of the American Smith Bristol Drug Company will be described.

ANALYSIS OF CALL FREQUENCY REQUIREMENTS—A CASE STUDY

The American Smith Bristol Drug Company produces fine pharmaceuticals which are distributed nationally and internationally through two independent sales organizations. Nationally, they distribute to relatively small accounts, selling through a wholesale distributor organization. The company employs a sales force of thirty missionary salesmen, who call upon consumers as well as distributors. The consumers include hospitals, city and state health services, clinics, other pharmaceutical companies, universities, and some research and development laboratories.

The company has regional sales managers, a home office sales manager, and an assistant manager. The basic problem in this area was identified as control of the salesmen. The salesmen were basically technical people with a minimum of sales experience. The firm was continually faced with the problem of determining how many salesmen would be needed to provide coverage of customers and potential customers.

The steps in determining an answer to this problem are:

1. Identify existing and potential customers.
2. Rank the customers in groups by profit contribution potential.
3. Determine a call frequency for each customer group.
4. Determine the total calls that must be made, on the basis of the number of customers by group and the related call frequency.
5. Determine the number of calls that one salesman can make in a year.
6. Determine the total number of salesmen needed.
7. Develop profitability by sales territory.

There are many sources for identifying customers and potential customers. Certainly the starting place is the internal data of the company. Accounts that have been sold to in the past or have been called upon can be classified as customers and potential customers. To assure complete coverage, other sources, such as census data, industry directories, and even the yellow pages of the telephone directory, are available.

After a listing of customers and prospects is made, a value or weight must be placed on each account. Sales can be correlated with size characteristics through existing corporate knowledge and available statistics. In the American Smith Bristol Drug Company, the firm's own sales statistics and the accounts in each territory were analyzed to determine customer potential. Plots were made on a graph on the basis of profit contribution per territory, and not on the basis of sales. Profit contribution potential was used to judge the importance of customers.

Exhibit 59 shows the analysis of profit contribution per account compared with the call frequency for the American Smith Bristol

ANALYSIS OF PROFIT CONTRIBUTION PER ACCOUNT
AND CALL FREQUENCY

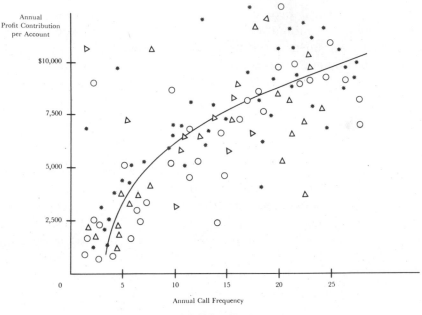

Exhibit 59

Drug Company. The accounts in the territories analyzed are plotted in varying symbols, and a line is judgmentally fitted to the plots. From this line we can determine a call frequency that will probably yield the profit contribution wanted, with the desired level of emphasis on key accounts.

To utilize the concept of customer/profit emphasis, customers and potential customers are grouped into A, B, C, and D classifications to determine a call frequency. Again profit contribution is the indicator used to determine whether an account belongs at an A or a D call frequency. In Exhibit 60, customer profitability is plotted by call frequency in the classes of profit contribution. Using as a critical point the marginal return per call, the point where the number of sales calls to a customer in a class peaks and starts to yield less profit contribution per call has been determined. As soon as the slope of the plotted line appears to fall off in any one customer class, the most desirable number of sales calls for that customer classification has been passed.

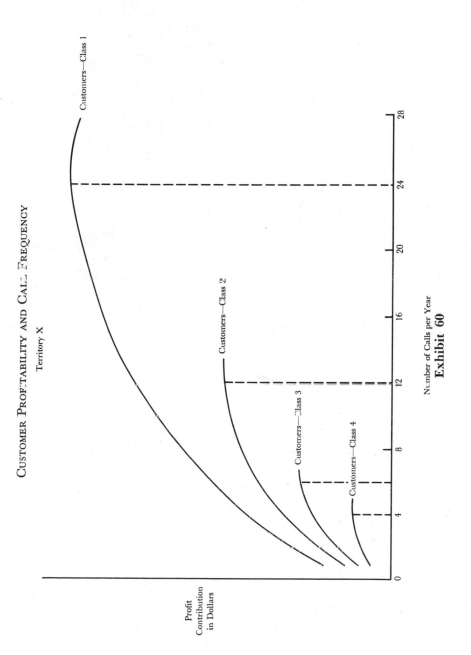

CUSTOMER PROFITABILITY AND CALL FREQUENCY

Territory X

Profit
Contribution
in Dollars

Customers—Class 1

Customers—Class 2

Customers—Class 3

Customers—Class 4

Number of Calls per Year

Exhibit 60

TOTAL CALL REQUIREMENT CALCULATION
Territory X

Class	Customer or Potential Customer Classification (Profit Contribution)	Actual		Plan				
				Call Frequency		Total Calls Required		
		No. of Customers	No. of Prospects	Planned Call Frequency	Planned Call Frequency	Calls/Year on Customers	Calls/Year on Prospects	Grand Total
1	Over $25,000	13	24	24	4	312	96	408
2	$10,000–25,000	29	88	12	3	348	264	612
3	$ 5,000–10,000	67	151	6	2	402	302	704
4	Less than $5,000	112	349	4	1	448	349	797
	Total	221	612	—	—	1,510	1,011	2,521

Exhibit 61

By placing these call frequencies in table form as shown in Exhibit 61, the total number of sales calls required in a territory can be determined. In Territory X, there are 13 existing customers whose profit contribution is $25,000 or more; this warrants their classification as Class 1 accounts. Additionally, there are 24 prospects warranting Class 1 consideration and emphasis. In this classification, management wants existing customers called upon 24 times a year, and prospects seen 4 times a year. By multiplying the number of customers and the number of prospects by the desired call frequency, the total calls to cover adequately Class 1 customers is determined to be 408 calls during the year. By repeating this computation for each class of customer, proper coverage of Territory X is determined to be 2,521 sales calls per year.

The next step is the determination of the number of calls a salesman can make in this territory. This requires working with field sales supervisors to determine the geographic characteristics and account and transportation problems encountered in covering the territory. For this territory, it has been determined that a salesman should make an average of 5 calls each day. This is a standard of 25 calls per week, and, working 250 days per year, a salesman should make 1,250 sales calls per year. Since the number of sales calls required in this territory is 2,521, it was concluded that an additional salesman should be added (see Exhibit 62).

STANDARD OF EFFORT, ONE SALESMAN
Territory X

Sales Calls Possible		
Per Day	Working Days/Year	Total per Year
5	250	1,250

Sales calls reported = 1,004

Sales calls feasible   = 1,250

Sales calls required = 2,521

Conclusion: Add an additional salesman.

Exhibit 62

The last step in the analysis is to determine whether the profit contribution from 1,250 sales calls could support the additional salesman. This computation is made by evaluating the sales per call and extending those sales by a gross profit contribution. Since the profit contribution computation was partially made in the original charting where sales call frequency was related to profit contribution, management felt confident that the addition of one salesman to this territory would add sufficient additional profit contribution to justify the additional salesmen. In this case, a new salesman was hired and there were boundary shifts of several territories.

The computation to determine the profit contribution and territory size to balance the territories is illustrated in the next case study, that of the Badger Light Company.

Sales Territory Evaluation—A Case Study

In the Badger Light Company, the vice president for sales has asked his wholesale sales manager for an analysis of salesmen's performance in the Midwest district, in seeking the answers to four basic questions:

1. Which salesmen have the best performances in their territories?
2. Which salesmen have the poorest performances?
3. Are our salesmen worth the money we pay them?
4. Do we have the right number of salesmen in this district?

Employing financial information available at corporate headquarters and statistical information obtained from the district offices, the wholesale sales manager worked with the controller's office to prepare the analysis shown in Exhibit 63.

In answering the questions regarding which salesmen have the best and which the poorest performances in their territories, Exhibit 63 indicates the performances of the eight salesmen in the district. For each territory the age of the salesman, the sales dollars, the territory potential in percent (the plan for the territory), and the differential performance index were computed. The variance from the PAR in dollars indicates that salesmen McBride, Venner,

ANALYSIS OF ACTUAL SALES PERFORMANCE vs. PAR

The Badger Light Company

Midwest District, 1968

Salesman	Age	Territory	Sales $(000)	Territory Potential* (Percent)	PAR for Territory $(000)	Performance Index	Variance from PAR over (under) $(000)
Kinney	38	Illinois (except Chicago)	$ 268	2.1	$ 425	63	$(157)
Larkin	62	Indiana	565	2.5	506	112	59
McBride	57	Northern Ohio	316	3.1	627	50	(311)
Newton	61	Southern Ohio	359	2.3	465	77	(106)
Osborne	63	Wisconsin	375	2.2	445	84	(70)
Sheppard	41	Kentucky	449	1.2	243	185	206
Tabor	53	Detroit, Michigan	403	2.2	445	91	(42)
Venner	28	Michigan (except Detroit)	211	2.1	425	50	(214)
Total			$ 2,946	17.7	$3,581	82	$(635)
Total U.S.			$20,229	100.0			

*Based on distribution of retail sales.

Exhibit 63

and Kinney are the poorest performers and that Sheppard and
Larkin have the best performances measured against PAR. In total
sales dollars Sheppard and Larkin also have the greatest amount
of sales.

Exhibits 64, 65, and 66 were prepared to answer the question
of whether the salesmen were worth the money they were being
paid.

In Exhibit 64, McBride and Venner have the lowest sales per 1
percent sales dollars of territorial potential. Kinney and Venner
had the lowest commission earnings in this district. Tabor, who
was under PAR by $42,000 (see Exhibit 63) and had a performance
index rate of 91 percent, had the third lowest rate of commission.
The fact that McBride, who was one of the three poorest-performing
salesmen, had the highest rate of commission (but not the highest
amount of commission dollars) led to the suspicion that the com-

ANALYSIS OF SALES COMMISSIONS VS. SALES POTENTIAL
The Badger Light Company
Midwest District, 1968

Salesman	Sales $(000)	Commission Rate (Percent)	Commission $(000)	Territory Potential* (Percent)	Sales per 1% of Potential $(000)
Kinney	$ 268	3.0	$ 8	2.1	$128
Larkin	565	7.8	44	2.5	226
McBride	316	8.2	26	3.1	102
Newton	359	8.1	29	2.3	156
Osborne	375	7.2	27	2.2	170
Sheppard	449	7.6	34	1.2	374
Tabor	403	6.9	28	2.2	183
Venner	211	4.7	10	2.1	100
Total	$ 2,946	7.0	$206	17.7	$166
Total U.S.	$20,229			100.0	

*On the basis of distribution of retail sales.

Exhibit 64

mission structure did not fairly reward sales performance. To sub-
stantiate this suspicion, an analysis was made of commissions earned
vs. profit contribution for the total district (see Exhibit 65). Kinney,
who earned 3.8 percent of the commissions, was responsible for sales
that yielded 10.6 percent of the profit contribution of the district.
While the performances of the other salesmen seemed to be bal-
anced, the fact that Kinney earned significantly less and Larkin
and Tabor earned significantly more in commissions than their
profit contribution percentages led to the sales, commissions,
and profit contributions analyses displayed in Exhibit 66. This
exhibit shows that the commission structure of the residential,
architectural, and industrial lines encouraged sales of products
where the profit contribution was poorest.

The chandelier line with only a 27.2 percent profit contribution
had a 7 percent commission rate, which encouraged sales effort,
while the close-to-wall line, with a 50.9 percent profit contribution
and a 3.9 percent commission rate, was not inducing salesmen's
efforts. As a result of these analyses, the commission structure was

ANALYSIS OF COMMISSIONS EARNED VS. PROFIT CONTRIBUTION
(expressed as percent of total district)
The Badger Light Company
Midwest District, 1968

Salesman	Commissions Earned, %	Profit Contribution, %
Kinney	3.8	10.6
Larkin	21.4	19.5
McBride	12.6	12.4
Newton	14.1	14.4
Osborne	13.2	13.5
Sheppard	16.6	16.5
Tabor	13.5	9.0
Venner	4.8	4.1
Total District, %	100.0	100.0

Exhibit 65

PRODUCT GROUP SALES ANALYSIS, SELECTED SALESMEN
The Badger Light Company
Midwest District, 1968

$(000)

				Residential					Architectural			Industrial Fluor.
				Chand.	Spots.	Clse-W	Outdoor	Circ. Rec.	Comm. Spot.	Rec. Fluor.	Wall	
Commission Rates, %				7.0	4.0	3.9	6.0	4.0	8.1	7.9	2.0	1.5
Profit Contribution, %				27.2	58.8	50.9	48.3	53.0	53.6	45.1	50.9	16.9

Salesman	*Age*	*Territory*	Total $(000)	Chand.	Spots.	Clse-W	Outdoor	Circ. Rec.	Comm. Spot.	Rec. Fluor.	Wall	Industrial Fluor.
SALES												
Kinney	38	Illinois	$ 268					$90	$ 10		$168	
Larkin	62	Indiana	565	$ 65				4	121	$372	3	
Tabor	53	Detroit	403	364	$ 1	$ 2	$36					
Venner	28	Michigan	211					11	5	3	32	$160
Total District			$2,946									
COMMISSIONS												
Kinney			$ 7.8					3.6	0.8		3.4	
Larkin			44.2	4.6				0.2	9.8	29.5	0.1	
Tabor			27.7	25.4		0.1	2.2					
Venner			9.8					0.4	0.4	0.2	6.4	2.4
Total District			$ 206.0									
PROFIT CONTRIBUTIONS												
Kinney			$ 138.6					47.6	5.4		85.6	
Larkin			253.9	17.7				2.1	64.8	167.8	1.5	
Tabor			117.6	99.0	0.6	1.0	17.0					
Venner			53.3					5.8	2.7	1.4	16.3	27.1
Total District			$1,303									

Exhibit 66

adjusted to balance profit contribution and desired sales effort.

To answer the question concerning the right number of sales-men in the districts, Exhibit 67 was prepared, comparing the sales potential per territory (the percentage of the total corporate sales potential for the territory) with the actual sales of that territory, expressed as sales per 1 percent of potential. Fewer sales dollars were being achieved per 1 percent of potential as territory potential increased. This discouraging revelation prompted management to ask for an analysis of optimum territory size, shown in Exhibit 68.

In Exhibit 68, the graph of Exhibit 67 is used to determine the potential sales effect that would occur by changing the number of salesmen to correspond with the relationship of sales assigned to the salesmen (one salesman per 1 percent equals 100 salesmen). The relationships of territory and division sizes are varied, and

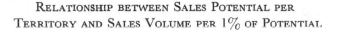

RELATIONSHIP BETWEEN SALES POTENTIAL PER
TERRITORY AND SALES VOLUME PER 1% OF POTENTIAL

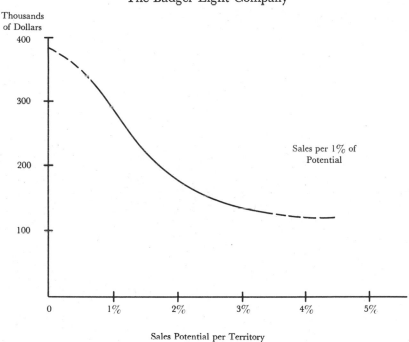

The Badger Light Company

Exhibit 67

PROJECTED TOTAL SALES VOLUME WITH VARYING NUMBERS OF SALESMEN
The Badger Light Company

Size of Individual Sales Territory, in Terms of Potential	Required Number of Salesmen	Sales per 1% of Potential $(000)	Estimated Total Sales Volume $(000)	Average Sales per Salesman $(000)	Profit Contribution 37.5% $(000)	Division Variable Expenses $(000) (Note A)	Division Promotional Expenses $(000) (Note B)	Division Earnings $(000)
.50%	200	$360	$36,000	$180	$13,500	$5,416	$424	$7,660
.67	150	340	34,000	227	12,750	4,062	424	8,264
1.00	100	295	29,500	295	11,062	2,708	424	7,930
1.25	80	250	25,000	313	9,375	2,167	424	6,784
1.54	65	220	22,000	338	8,250	1,760	424	6,066
1.67	60	202	20,200	336	7,565	1,625	424	5,506
2.00	50	170	17,000	340	6,375	1,354	424	4,597
2.50	40	145	14,500	363	5,438	1,084	424	3,930
3.33	30	130	13,000	433	4,875	813	424	3,638

Note A. Wholesale Division Expenses:

Total expenses $2,049

Promotional expenses 424

$1,625 ÷ 60 salesmen = $27,083/salesman

Note B. Promotional Expenses:

Consumer publications $ 360

Direct mail 58

Shows 6

$ 424

Assumptions:

1. 37.5% profit contribution.
2. All divisional expenses related to sales other than promotional expenses vary directly with the number of salesmen.

Exhibit 68

alternative territory sizes are analyzed. Variable expenses of $1,625,000 are related to a portion of sales at each level of volume, and a constant promotional expense figure of $424,000 is used. The indication is that earnings are best with 150 salesmen, and sales total $34,000,000. At this level the earnings are $8,264,000. The sales volume of $34,000,000 represents an increase of approximately $7,000,000 over last year's sales volume.

After reviewing these figures the sales vice president decided to increase the sales force to 150 men, on the basis of the information in Exhibit 68 and his assumption that he could improve the performance indicated by the solid line in Exhibit 67. He believed that with the increased number of salesmen, with each salesman responsible for 67 percent of the total corporate potential, the sales graph slope would be drastically improved. He was not a wishful thinker. Today the company is well on the way to his goal.

There are many ways of measuring sales within a district or territory. The ability to compare territorial results is a powerful weapon in business analysis. To compare results at the profit contribution level adds a supervisory dimension which allows the manager to move closer to the company's performance goals. Sales results can and must be related to profit goals. The ability to convey to the sales force the impact and influence of sales results on profit is often lacking in modern corporate life. By utilizing marginal analysis concepts and profit contribution figures, this dimension can be restored.

Chapter IX

Pricing

SOME OF the greatest rewards from obtaining marginal income information can be realized in the pricing function. Indeed, if there were no other justification for the marginal income approach, the ability to determine price/cost relationships would justify the rearranging of accounting statements into marginal and incremental cost and revenue formats.

Pricing is one of the most important decisions in the life of a business. It recurs numerous times in business management, and during the life of any product there are at least four distinct types of pricing decisions:

1. New product prices.
2. Price changes.
3. Product line interrelationships.
4. Liquidation pricing.

The new product price decision requires definition of a company's pricing objectives and of objectives set for the product line and the product. In a recent Brookings Institution study, "Pricing in Big Business," by A. D. H. Kaplan, J. B. Dirlam, and R. F. Lanzillotti, four pricing objectives were most frequently cited as the goals to be attained in product pricing. These objectives were: pricing to achieve a target return on investment; stabilization of the price and margin relationship; pricing to receive a targeted market share; and pricing to meet competition.

Unless a company obtains a pricing level that allows it to cover full costs and to provide contribution in the long run, it will fail. However, for any one product a short-range decision may involve the interaction of many relationships, and management can price at many discretionary levels. In the short run a price may be a proportion of total costs, incremental costs, or conversion costs. The short-run managed price may be related to achieving a definite market share. This type of decision depends upon the stage of product development of the competitive intensity being encountered or expected. The short-run pricing objective selected for a product may result in low-level pricing to gain mass distribution, or at a high level to "skim" a market. A "skimming" price plan may be selected to attain a maximum opportunistic profit during the first stages of product introduction, leaving room to drop prices and become mass marketed later in the product's life cycle.

The price change decision, which is a daily market-response situation in some industries (for example, the petroleum industry), is an infrequent, oligopolistically managed decision in other industries. The aggressiveness of one company or the defensive nature of its competitors in the market is often well known within an industry. The choice of a market posture is generally dictated by management's knowledge of the company's cost structure. A secure management, knowing that its costs are in line with those encountered in the industry, and knowing that the price/cost relationship allows room for maneuvering, can take an aggressive market position. The insecure company, unsure of cost or profit relationships, often is responsive or defensive in its pricing policies.

An example of aggressiveness versus responsive pricing can be seen in the oil industry. "Crude rich" companies, those who own adequate crude oil reserves, with a fully integrated well-to-market setup, are often market leaders in setting gasoline retail price structures within geographical areas. "Crude poor" firms, which do not own sufficient amounts of crude oil to supply all their marketing needs, often adopt a defensive pricing strategy, choosing to emphasize service or other marketing characteristics rather than price.

In the product-line interrelationship decision, cost of manufacture and distribution can be used with great sophistication, as cost estimates are used to select the most profitable pricing pattern. This allows for products to be designed to sell at various pricing points. The "full lining" concept evolves. Often the incremental stepup in the price line more than covers the cost of the additional or new features.

An example of price lining occurred when the first electric portable typewriter was introduced by the SCM Corporation. SCM introduced four portable electric typewriters ranging from $149.50 to $199.50 in list price. They all had a manual carriage return. The company's smallest fully electric nonportable typewriter (with an electric carriage return) was priced at $250.00 and was considered an office model. The steps, or price points, within the price line progressed from a "stripped down" model to one designed for a price point just beneath the "stripped down" model of the office or nonportable series. An interesting incident occurred when a competitor, the Royal Typewriter Company, introduced its first portable electric typewriter with a list price of $199.50, equal to the SCM top-of-the-line portable price. Royal's typewriter had an electrified carriage return and tabulator key. Apparently Royal's tactic was to equal SCM's top-of-the-line price and compete on the basis of the additional features of the office model. The interrelationships among the models and prices of Royal and SCM formed a price line pattern wherein features and prices of one line would be compared with the features and prices of the other line. A pricing decision made by either competitor on a model would interreact and cause evaluations of position up and down the competitive line.

The fourth type of price decision occurs during the liquidation or phasing-out stage of the product's life cycle. Here again, cost enters the price decision. If the product is being phased out in an orderly manner, the product will be priced to return at least its marginal or out-of-pocket costs. Normally, a contribution will be expected from the product even during the phaseout. In other cases where the product has not been successful and management desires to leave the market, particularly when the product has a demand that is fleeting, management will often consider the direct costs already in the product as "sunk" costs and "dump" the product onto the market, thereby taking any income received from the liquidation of the remaining stock as a recovery of working capital.

The fact that a product isn't priced once, launched, and left alone contributes to the dynamics of the pricing decision. There are numerous corporate objectives, interrelationships, and traditional means of pricing to be considered at all times. Some factors, other than cost, affecting price are, of course, supply and demand, opportunity, investment, competition, the method of product distribution, sales promotion and advertising, government, and combinations of these factors. Indeed, the relationships among product prices are almost never determined mechanistically by cost difference. Joel Dean, of Columbia University, points out that considering cost alone is a fatal error in sensible, product-line pricing. "Unit profit margins over arbitrarily allocated full cost may be tolerable in inflation, but the problem of many firms is to limit profits rather than maximize them. But during periods of declining business activity, this policy is usually indefensible. The company's alternatives, if it does not get a full margin price on a particular product, are then sharply different from boom periods." In other words, in the face of market realities, mechanistic pricing on the basis of costs, particularly full costs, is an unreal approach. There are too many factors other than costs to be considered. If this is so, what good is cost information?

In pricing, cost information can be used to do the following:

1. Measure the effect of alternative strategies.
2. Establish decision parameters, such as the lowest price at which a company will be willing to sell a product and the magnitude of profit to take in an opportunistic situation.
3. Forecast reactions of customers and competitors.
4. Defend against Government action such as a Robinson-Patman Act cost defense, whereby costs may be used to justify discriminatory pricing.

Using Marginal Costs

Marginal costs are appropriate for use in the first three of the four uses of cost information. In the fourth, the Government demands pricing based on fully absorbed costs; therefore, this fact is used in Robinson-Patman Act cost defenses, ICC rate cases, and other appearances or defenses of actions before Government bodies. However, in the decision-making process, which is common to the first three uses, marginal costing is essential.

The information given a manager will, of course, influence his pricing decision. If the information is based on fully absorbed costs, and a bid decision is being made, judgment will be affected, and the bidder may misconstrue the cost effect of the sale. This is shown in Exhibit 69, where a product selling for one dollar, on a sale of 20,000 units, contributes $6,600 on a marginal basis, but shows a $2,000 loss when fully absorbed costs are used. If a businessman were faced with a one-time sale decision, he might misconstrue the fully absorbed information to tell him not to make a sale of the 20,000 units. This decision would bypass profit contribution of $6,600. In this simplified illustration, the first value of marginal costing in the pricing area is illustrated. It is a decision-making device that isolates the effect of a management action.

The so-called break-even analysis, shown in Exhibit 70, can be constructed when marginal costs are known. Many analyses can be portrayed in this type of presentation. Total demand at various price levels and the effects of several sales forecasts can be plotted. An example of this is the demand analysis for a product priced at $10, $12, $15, $17, and $20, which has been computed and plotted. The highest profit contribution, or marginal revenue, will be realized at a $12 price level. Management can observe the effects of the alternate prices and can see the "sensitivity" or "downside" risk of other price levels.

Using marginal cost information, management can analyze product line profit contribution and ask hypothetical questions. An example of this is given in Exhibit 71, where the effects of a 20 percent higher price or a 15 percent lower price are shown as responses to a competitive action.

In Exhibit 71, forecasts of unit sales volume at the new price levels are made, and the incremental profit contributions are com-

FULLY ABSORBED U.S. MARGINAL COST CALCULATIONS

Fully Absorbed Costs

Proposed bid price	$ 1.00
Factory cost (fully absorbed)	.95
Add: Shipping costs	.15
Total cost	1.10
Loss per unit	.10
Units sold	20,000
Total loss	$ 2,000

Marginal Cost

Proposed bid price	$ 1.00
Marginal costs	
Direct materials	.20
Direct labor	.15
Variable overhead	.17
Shipping charge	.15
Total marginal costs	.67
Profit contribution per unit	.33
Units sold	20,000
Contribution to corporate overhead and profits made by this sale	$ 6,600 *

*This contribution would not have been made to corporate overhead and profits if the sales had not been made.

Exhibit 69

puted. Management is able to determine its risk under the alternate courses of action. At a 20 percent higher price, selling 20 percent fewer tapes, the Acme Record Company would realize more in gross and net profit contributions and higher gross and net profit contribution percentages to sales, assuming the same level of specific programmed expenses. Indeed, in a situation similar to this, a firm upgraded its pricing and product lines, the brand involved became the most prestigious in its field, and the company realized greater profits. The alarming effect of a lower price, with the same variable costs and programmed expense structure, can be observed. With a

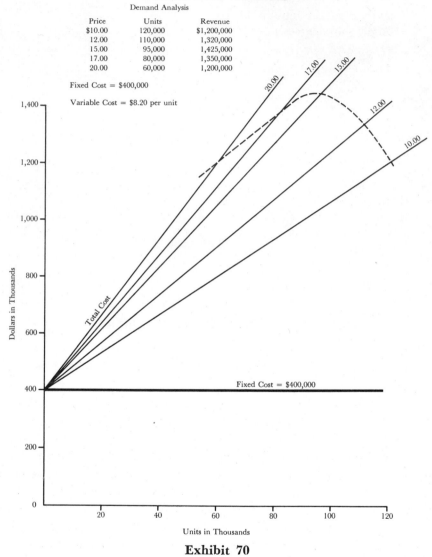

"Break Even" Analysis

Demand Analysis

Price	Units	Revenue
$10.00	120,000	$1,200,000
12.00	110,000	1,320,000
15.00	95,000	1,425,000
17.00	80,000	1,350,000
20.00	60,000	1,200,000

Fixed Cost = $400,000

Variable Cost = $8.20 per unit

Fixed Cost = $400,000

Dollars in Thousands

Total Cost

Units in Thousands

Exhibit 70

PRODUCT LINE PROFIT CONTRIBUTIONS
Acme Record Company
Product Lines

	Tapes	*Cartridges*	*Records*	*Total*
Sales	$600,000	$200,000	$200,000	$1,000,000
Variable costs	400,000	90,000	110,000	600,000
Gross profit contribution	200,000	110,000	90,000	400,000
Gross profit contribution % to sales	33 .3	55	45	40
Specific programmed costs	100,000	40,000	10,000	150,000
Profit contribution	$100,000	$ 70,000	$ 80,000	$ 250,000
Profit contribution % to sales	16.7	35	40	25
General proposed cost				75,000
Standby costs				125,000
Operating profit				$ 50,000
Operating profit % to sales				5

Effect of Price Changes on Tape Line

	Present Price	*20% Higher*	*15% Lower*
Unit sales	$100,000	$ 80,000	$125,000
Unit price	6.00	7.20	5.10
Variable unit cost	4.00	4.00	4.00
Sales	600,000	576,000	637,000
Variable cost	400,000	320,000	500,000
Gross profit contribution	200,000	256,000	137,000
Gross profit contribution % to sales	33.3	44.5	31.5
Specific programmed expense	100,000	100,000	100,000
Profit contribution	$100,000	$156,000	$ 37,000
Profit contribution % to sales	16.7	27.1	5.8

Exhibit 71

15 percent lower price and a 25 percent increase in volume, the tape line's gross profit contribution to sales drops by 46.5 percent, and the line's net profit contribution to sales falls by 63 percent. This type of gaming is possible only if marginal income figures are available to marketing management.

Another use of marginal cost information is in pricing for a target return on investment percentage. The technique involved is shown in Exhibit 72, where a break-even line is portrayed, and the line necessary for a projected return on investment or to satisfy a plan is also shown. Using this, management can trace the point where marginal income passes the break-even point and produces the target or planned return on the investment in the product line. The determination of this return target will be discussed in the next chapter.

Marginal costing permits alternative statements of product-price relationship to be exhibited for management decision making. While recognizing that a strict "by the numbers" or mechanical approach of relating price to cost can be dangerous, a marginal price approach permits sophistication in the selection of those costs that are important to a specific pricing decision. The main job of costs in pricing is helping to select the most profitable price pattern to implement management policies. Incremental costs are most appropriate for this because they best portray demand-cost relationships.

THE ROBINSON-PATMAN ACT

In 1936 Congress passed the Robinson-Patman Act. It is this Act that is generally of concern in pricing decision making. Within the Act are provisions that make it illegal to charge different prices to different customers for products of like grade and quality if the differential in price tends to injure competition. The Act does not necessarily restrict price differences to customers who are not in competition, but price differentials that tend to injure competing customers are illegal. While there are other provisions of the Act concerning advertising allowances, discounts, and trade restrictions, the price differential area is of interest in this chapter.

Within the Act, a seller, if called to justify a price action, has two acceptable defenses. Either he can prove that a lower price was granted in "good faith" to meet the price policy of a competitor, quite often a very difficult point to prove, or he must prove that his price policy reflects an actual difference in cost. There have been very few cases on record where sellers have used the cost defense in a Robinson-Patman action successfully.

PRICING FOR TARGET RETURN ON ASSETS MANAGED

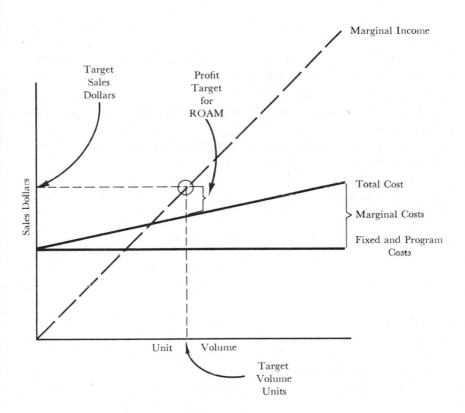

Exhibit 72

There are several reasons for this. First of all, there is little knowledge of successful cost defenses. If a company's costs justify its actions to the FTC accountants, the case will not often reach the courts, and therefore not become part of the public record. This has resulted in a lack of generally available information about successful cost defenses, and without this knowledge many companies are not willing to try the defense. Second, it can be expensive to cost-justify an action. We believe the point has been well made in this book that normal, custodial accounting records do not provide costs in the detail required to be attributed to a specific management decision that would be necessary to justify an action under the Robinson-Patman Act. To incur the cost necessary to reorganize information in a form required for a cost defense is often less expensive than submitting to a consent order and giving up a trade practice, which usually means lowering prices to many smaller customers.

The full absorption cost practice is demanded in Robinson-Patman Act defenses. In order to organize for a cost defense, or merely to cost-justify an action, the cost information building blocks necessary to implement the marginal costing concepts previously discussed must be available, so that costs can be distributed to the products or customers in question. In a cost justification action all related costs must be distributed to all customers, thereby fully absorbing all related costs into the customer or product-line structure.

Customers must be classified into homogeneous groupings that coincide with the pricing policies under question. The costs of manufacturing and distribution are then allocated to the customer groupings on the basis of the activities or functions applicable to the customer groups in question.

The concept of a service "unit" has been developed to distribute costs to the function. A service unit is a distribution base such as a unit of transportation, warehousing, selling, technical service, or other applicable distribution base that is used to segment a cost and apply the cost to the object of measurement. These service-unit allocation bases can be dollars of sales, miles driven by a salesman, square feet of warehousing space, or other factors that the person assigning the costs deems applicable in the allocation process.

Costs in natural classifications are then allocated to customer groups on the basis of the service units and data, or studies of volume of units by customer group. This is shown in Exhibits 73 and 74.

In Exhibit 73, a cost allocation justifying a quantity discount based upon order size is shown. This and the example presented

COST ALLOCATION EXAMPLES UNDER THE ROBINSON-PATMAN ACT

Discount on the Basis of Order Size
2% on 13–24 units
3% on 25–48 units
5% on 49 or more units

Samples of cost allocations
Full cost of
    Order handling $.78 per order*
    Processing, payment, and auditing of freight bill $.47 per order*

*On the basis of sample of orders, specific work measurement techniques, and actual accounting costs.

			Costs per Unit	
Order Group	*Average Order Size*	*Order Handling*	*Freight Processing, etc.*	*Freight†*
0–12 units	4 units	$.195	$.118	$.371
13–24	16	.049	.029	.293
25–48	34	.023	.014	.238
49 and over	60	.013	.008	.191

†On the basis of average shipment sizes, distribution of shipping points, and sampling of freight bills.

		Per Unit		
Order Group	*Total Costs*	*Cost Savings over Previous Order Group*	*Sales Price*	*Price Difference*
0–12 units	$8.07	—	$10.00	—
13–24	7.49	$.58	9.80	$.20
25–48	7.21	.28	9.70	.10
49 and over	7.00	.21	9.50	.20

Exhibit 73

in Exhibit 74 do not use data taken from actual cost defense cases, but the methodology has been successfully used in cost defenses.

COST ALLOCATION EXAMPLES UNDER THE ROBINSON-PATMAN ACT

Discount on the Basis of Annual Purchases
2% on $5,000–$9,999
3% on $10,000–$25,000
4% on over $25,000

Direct selling expense:
- Considered only cost group to vary with annual purchases.
- Allocated to customers on basis of number of calls per customer.
- Total expense = $1,000,000.
- Total calls = 40,000.
- Expense per call = $25.00.

Customer Group	Sales Range	Average Gross Sales per Customer	Average Calls per Customer*	Average Gross Sales per Call Dollars	Units	Cost per Unit Sold
A	Over $25,000	$53,000	26/yr.	$2,040	204	$.123
B	$10,000–$25,000	17,000	15/yr.	1,130	113	.221
C	$5,000–$9,999	7,000	9/yr.	780	78	.321
D	$0–$4,999	1,500	4/yr.	380	38	.658

*On the basis of sample of call reports.

Customer Group	Sales Range	Net Price per Unit Dollars	Difference	Cost per Unit Dollars	Difference
A	Over $25,000	$ 9.60	$.10	$.123	$.098
B	$10,000–$25,000	9.70	.10	.221	.100
C	$5,000–$9,999	9.80	.20	.321	.337
D	$0–$4,999	10.00	—	.658	—

Exhibit 74

In Exhibit 73 the full costs of order handling and processing, payment, and audit of freight bills are arrived at by sampling orders, performing a work measurement study, and distributing actual accounting costs into the costs of order handling. The cost of processing, payment, and audit of freight are based upon the average shipment sizes, the distribution of shipping points, and a sampling of freight bills. By determining the costs per unit within four order groups, a price discount structure of $0.20, $0.10, and $0.20 from the base price of $10.00 appears to be justifiable, on the basis of total costs of handling and processing the average order sizes within the four order groups.

In Exhibit 74, to arrive at a cost justification for annual quantity discounts, the direct selling expense for four customer groups has been calculated. Based upon the sales range within the groups and the number of direct sales calls required per year to service the group, a direct sales cost per unit sold within each group has been computed. When this cost per unit sold is applied to the sales structure, the 2 percent, 3 percent, and 4 percent annual quantity discount structure appears to be more than justified by cost.

Use of the concepts of cost defense, while applicable to the Robinson-Patman Act, also indicates the concepts of distribution cost analysis where the full costs of transportation, distribution, and marketing are often computed on a functional basis to determine the most profitable channels of distribution. The cost defense concepts are applicable in actions involving the Government, and are shown in this book for that reason. They should be used carefully for decision making, as the behavior pattern of the allocated portion of costs often has not been adequately portrayed to the decision maker. Distribution cost analysis is a valued discipline when properly used and when costs within the distribution are shown in a manner that indicates the consequences of a particular decision.

Chapter X

Return on Investment for Marketers

THE CONCEPT of return on investment has been recognized as a major tool for financial evaluation and capital planning for many years. Alfred P. Sloan, in his book *My Years with General Motors*, comments that "no other financial principle with which I am acquainted serves better than rate of return as an objective aid to business judgment." Although return on investment is probably less frequently applied to marketing management applications than to other areas of business, the principles and techniques involved are as valid in marketing management as in any other segment of a business. Perhaps one of the reasons these techniques have not been used as frequently in marketing is that financial records data have rarely had the necessary detail for marketing and sales investment analyses. In this chapter the basic principles of return on investment will be outlined, and special emphasis will be given to marketing management use.

156

Applications of return on investment can be divided into two major classifications. The first is the measurement of historical financial performance. This analysis may be made for the whole company or for a specific part of the business, such as a division or sales function. A similar analysis may be prepared for a nonfunctional classification, such as product line or channel of distribution. Return on investment provides a useful quantitative method for comparing the experiences of like businesses or segments of a business. The second major use of the return-on-investment technique is application to planning and capital investment. In this case, return-on-investment analysis allows the user to reduce the expected financial results of alternative decisions to a common denominator. Comparison can then be made between investments in relation to established objectives and goals.

Exhibit 75 illustrates graphically these two major uses of return on investment. Although we have a "chicken and egg" problem in determining which comes first—planning for the future or evaluation of the past—it is more convenient here to establish the principles of R.O.I. as a measurement of performance and then investigate the techniques for analysis of future plans and budgets.

RETURN ON EQUITY

One of the immediate questions that must be answered in dealing with the return-on-investment concept is, "Which investment is involved?" One of the fundamental areas of investment is that of equity—stockholders' equity or the owner's investment in the business. The return on these investments is obtained by dividing earnings by the investment of the partners or shareholders plus the earnings retained in the business. This measure of return is of considerable importance to investors. However, using this base for a measure of return ignores the fact that others may have substantial investments in the company in the form of long- or short-term loans and current trade payables. In addition, it would be difficult, if not impossible, to segment the investment of equity into the various functional and nonfunctional segments of the business so that an individual manager's or division's functional performance could be measured. Therefore, for the purpose of measuring man-

Return-on-Investment Concepts

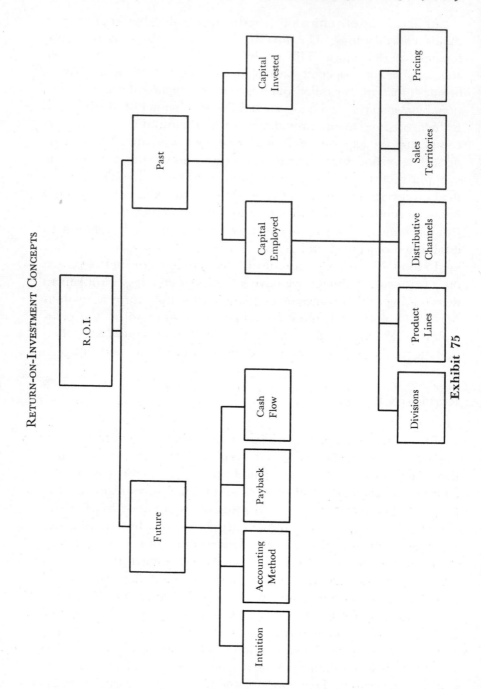

Exhibit 75

agement, it is more useful to utilize a base of total assets employed in the corporation. "Assets employed" is a value obtained directly from the balance sheet of the operation and through detailed subsidiary accounting records. Throughout this chapter, when reference is made to return on investment, it will refer to assets employed, although investment connotes a different base than the assets.

RETURN ON ASSETS EMPLOYED

Information regarding stockholders' equity positions is found on the right-hand side of the balance sheet with the liabilities of the company. Exhibit 76 is a simplified balance sheet showing the financial position of the Badger Light Company as of December 31, 1968. To obtain the value of the assets employed, observe the left-hand side of the balance sheet, where the company's various categories of assets may be found. By looking into the company's books of account and the manner in which these assets are distributed among divisions, the investments by product line, territory, or channel of distribution may be determined. Beneath the balance sheet in Exhibit 76, the simplified calculation of return on investment on the basis of pretax return on equity and of assets employed can be seen.

All of the information required to calculate the return on investment was not obtained from the balance sheet in Exhibit 76. The earnings portion of the calculation must come from the profit-and-loss statement for the period ending as of the date of the balance sheet. In fact, one of the strengths of the return-on-investment analysis is that it brings together aspects of these two financial documents into one indicator.

RETURN-ON-INVESTMENT CONCEPT

The return-on-investment concept may be further expanded into two performance measures. This is illustrated as follows:

$$\frac{\text{Earnings}}{\text{Assets Employed}} = \frac{\text{Earnings}}{\text{Sales}} \times \frac{\text{Sales}}{\text{Assets Employed}}$$

RETURN-ON-INVESTMENT ANALYSIS
The Badger Light Company
Statement of Financial Position
December 31, 1968

Assets

Current assets
Cash	$ 756,427
Accounts receivable	6,322,113
Inventories	7,144,567
Prepaid expenses	637,521
Total current assets	$14,860,628
Property, plant, and equipment	3,426,531
Other investments	1,050,000
Other assets	934,621
	$20,271,780

Liabilities and Owners' Equity

Current liabilities
Trade accounts payable	$ 2,321,333
Accrued wages and salaries	647,821
Federal income taxes payable	1,473,198
Other liabilities	693,114
Total current liabilities	$ 5,135,466
Stockholders' equity	
Common stock	1,200,000
Retained earnings	13,936,314
	$20,271,780

Return-on-Investment Measures

$$\text{Pretax return on equity} = \frac{\text{Earnings}}{\text{Equity}} = \frac{1,810}{15,136} = 12.0\%$$

$$\text{*Return on assets employed} = \frac{\text{Earnings}}{\text{Employed}} = \frac{1,810}{20,272} = 8.9\%$$

*Average assets for the year may be used. The average assets may be accurately shown at December 31—one point of the year. However, end-of-the-year assets are adequate for this simplified example.

Exhibit 76

Return on assets employed is actually a combination of earnings, as a percentage of sales profit (or margin), and sales, as a percentage of capital employed, often referred to as asset or capital turnover. The segregation of these elements of return on investment is important because it is possible to influence return by changing either turnover or the profit percentage.

It is of interest to look at the same formula modified to give the return on equity: *

$$\frac{\text{Earnings}}{\text{Equity}} = \frac{\text{Earnings}}{\text{Sales}} \times \frac{\text{Sales}}{\text{Assets Employed}} \times \frac{\text{Assets Employed}}{\text{Equity}}$$

Expressed this way, the formula includes the additional factor of capital employed as a percentage of equity. This factor, sometimes known as the capital leverage, is very important to the investor because it measures the amount of outside capital that is being employed in relation to his own.

Exhibit 77 illustrates the use of the return-on-investment formula to analyze and compare the financial performance of the Badger Light Company with the performances of two competitors. Although Badger Light's income as a percentage of sales is higher than those of its two competitors, Company C, with a turnover of 2.0, is able to obtain a return on assets employed of 10 percent compared with 8.9 percent for Badger Light.

As indicated previously, elements of cost that influence earnings and the investment in various assets may be further classified into categories related to functional responsibilities; to subelements of operations, such as a division; or to product lines, channel of distribution, or other characteristics that may merit detailed evaluation. Exhibit 78 shows the relationships between these costs and investment for the Badger Light Company as a whole. Similar charts could be constructed for other functions or areas of interest.

Uses of Return on Investment

Many techniques have been suggested for application of the return-on-investment method of evaluation to responsibilities below the level of top management. It might be useful to evaluate the return on investment achieved for sales territories, as is done in

ANALYSIS OF RETURN ON ASSETS EMPLOYED

	Badger Light Company	Company B	Company C
1. Sales	$27,000	$50,000	$10,000
2. Income	1,810	3,000	500
3. Assets employed	20,272	50,000	5,000
4. Income as % of sales	6.7%	6.0%	5.0%
5. Turnover (line 1/line 3)	1.33	1.0	2.0
6. Return on assets employed (line 4 × line 5)	8.9%	6.0%	10.0%

Exhibit 77

Exhibit 79. From the sales and expense records, revenues and expenses have been obtained that relate specifically to Territories A and B. From sales revenue the standard variable costs (discussed in previous chapters) have been subtracted to arrive at a standard profit contribution for each territory. From the standard profit contributions the specific territorial expenses have been removed to determine territorial earnings. From the asset accounts, the accounts receivable related directly to each territory and the inventories specifically assigned to the territories have been shown. An examination of sales and earnings indicates that Territory A has, through higher sales and better mix, produced a higher earnings percentage. But the investment required to achieve this sales and earnings record is over twice that required in Territory B, and the result is that Territory B is able to generate better than twice the return on investment.

To relate performances in Territories A and B with the rest of the company, the same exercise must be carried out for all territories, and their totals must be related to other expenses and corporate assets not specifically assignable to territorial management (see Exhibit 80). It should be noted that the return on investment for the territories is not necessarily the same as that experienced by the corporation as a whole, and rightfully so, because some assets cannot be directly assigned to sales responsibilities or "down" to the

Formula Chart

The Badger Light Company

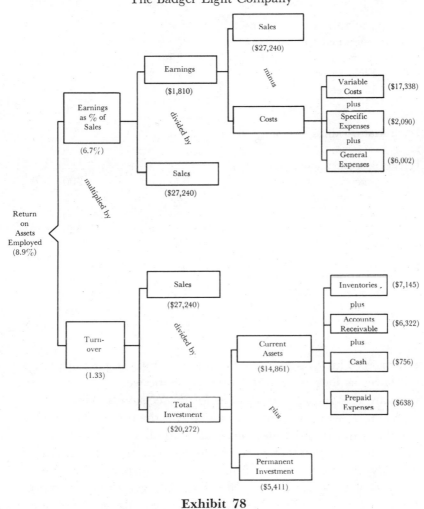

Exhibit 78

TERRITORIAL RETURN ON INVESTMENT

	Territory A	Territory B
Sales	$2,400	$1,500
Less: Standard variable costs	1,600	1,125
Standard profit contribution	800 (33%)	375 (25%)
Less: Specific territorial expenses		
Salesmen compensation	250	100
Travel and entertainment	75	25
Field sales office expenses	50	25
Bad debts	25	—
	400	150
Territorial earnings	400	225
Territorial investments		
Accounts receivable	800	200
Inventories	800	200
	$1,600	$ 400
Earnings as % of sales	16.7%	15.0%
Turnover	1.5	3.75
Territorial % return on investment	25.0%	56.3%

Exhibit 79

territories. This evaluation is useful in comparing territorial performance, as long as unusual differences between or among territories are recognized and allowed for in decision making.

A similar analysis may be made for product lines. This is shown in Exhibit 81. It is readily seen that a number of factors affect the return on investment achieved in the segment of the business evaluated. By the same token, emphasis on control, or increase and decrease of these factors, enables the manager to effect improvements in return on investment. Sales price, mix, and volume increase with no increase in capital utilized will favorably affect the return on investment. Reduction in cost and expenses without an increase in sales or a reduction in the level of capital required to

SETTING THE RETURN-ON-INVESTMENT TARGET

Territory Marketing Information

	Sales	*Territorial Earnings*	*Territorial Investment*	*Territorial R.O.I.*
Territory A	$ 2,400	$ 400	$ 1,600	25.0%
Territory B	1,500	225	400	56.3%
All territories	$27,240	$7,810	$13,467	58.0%

Other Corporate Data

General expenses	6,000
Corporate earnings	$1,810
Corporate assets (excluding accounts receivable and inventories)	6,805
Corporate assets employed	$20,272
Corporate return on assets employed	8.9%

Exhibit 80

maintain the sales level will favorably affect the return on investment realized.

The determination of return on investment is an extremely useful measure of performance between or among comparable units. It is important that each unit have identifiable profit or earnings and specific expenses and capital investment that can be related to the unit measured, with reasonable reliability. Caution must be taken in using this measure lest the units evaluated or compared are not related to a degree sufficient to make the returns comparable. For example, the return on investment of a product line is not necessarily comparable with the return on investment of a sales territory. Nor is the return on investment of a product line necessarily comparable with the return on investment of a division producing that product. For effective performance evaluation, goals for return on investment must be established for each segment of the corporation being measured.

Use of return on investment as a selling tool. With methods similar to those already described, a product can be evaluated for a prospective purchaser in terms of its forecast benefits. Many products are sold only on the basis of benefits to be achieved over products or equipment presently in service. The next major section of this chapter, "Methods of Analysis," illustrates several approaches to the application of return on investment to project evaluation, as a decision-making or selling tool.

Use of return on investment for evaluating proposed strategy. As in the product line return-on-investment technique illustrated in Exhibit 81, return-on-investment technique can be effectively used for evaluating projects and proposals to be "sold" to decision makers within the corporation. In those instances where a project promises to change additional profit contribution, and where the specific ex-

STATEMENT OF EARNINGS, BY PRODUCT
The Badger Light Company
Year Ended December 31, 1968

	Total Company	Residential Products	Architectural Products	Industrial Products
Sales	$27,240	$4,560	$18,398	$4,282
Less: Standard variable costs	17,338	2,630	10,848	3,860
Profit contribution	9,902	1,930	7,500	422
Profit contribution percentage	36.4	42.3	41.0	9.9
Less: Specific product expenses				
Selling	1,385	526	674	185
Advertising	265	115	75	75
Promotion and trade shows	360	360	—	—
Administration	80	27	51	2
	2,090	1,028	800	262
Product earnings	$ 7,812	$ 902	$ 6,750	$ 160
Product investment				
Accounts received	$ 6,322	$1,267	$ 4,153	$ 902
Inventory	7,145	1,023	5,340	582
	$13,467	$2,290	$ 9,493	$1,484
Earnings as % of sales	28.7%	19.8%	36.7%	3.7%
Turnover	2.0	2.0	1.9	2.9
Product return on investment	58.0	39.4	71.1	10.8

Exhibit 81

penses and the specific assets related to the project may be identified, the techniques of return on investment may be applied. Projects as diverse as the introduction of a new product line and the purchase of a piece of capital equipment can be effectively analyzed in this manner. Exhibit 82, an evaluation of product planning strategy, illustrates an application of return-on-investment analysis.

On a rather simplified basis the concept of return on investment has been defined, and several broad uses of the technique have been illustrated. There are, however, major considerations in the application of return on investment which have not been covered. In evaluating past performance, for instance, it is relatively easy to insure that a common basis is established for comparison among the units to be measured. The value of money over a period of time, incremental investments, or the fact that incomes are not necessarily received during the same period that investments are made have not been taken into account. For those utilizations of the return-on-investment concept which entail a measurement of expected results in the future, such as using the return on investment as a selling tool or choosing the best alternatives for making capital investment, there is a need to recognize these additional considerations in the calculations. The difficulty in obtaining valid data is one consideration. Also, in projecting future benefits from capital investment by the return on investment method there are noncash expenses such as depreciation and amortization which also must be recognized because of their effect as a tax shield for the corporation. In the following sections several methods for applying return on investment for evaluating and comparing potential alternative investments will be shown.

METHODS OF ANALYSIS

The job of forecasting and planning for any portion of a business is difficult and subject to many errors and inaccuracies. This is primarily because there are few certain elements affecting a forecast. The use of return-on-investment analysis to assist in decision making for planning and budgeting does not change forecasting inaccuracies or relieve the burden of planning without an abundance of facts. However, the return-on-investment concept does

APPLICATION OF RETURN-ON-INVESTMENT ANALYSIS

		Product A	Product B	Product C	Total	General Program and Standby	Net Earnings Before Tax	Assets Employed	Return on Assets Before Tax
1968	Selling Price per Unit	$10.00	$80.00	$60.00					
	Profit Contribution %	20	40	30	27				
	Actual volume-units	400	20	40					
	Sales	$4,000	$1,600	$2,400	$8,000				
	Profit contribution	800	640	720	2,160				
	Specific prog. and standby exp.	100	260	200	560				
		$ 700	$ 380	$ 520	$1,600	$1,120	$480	$3,600	13%
Strategy A	Selling Price per Unit	$12.00	$80.00	$54.00					
	Profit Contribution %	33.3	40	26	31.5				
	Expected volume-units	333	16	60					
	Sales	$4,000	$1,280	$3,240	$8,520				
	Profit contribution	1,333	512	840	2,685				
	Specific prog. and standby exp.	200	160	265	325				
		$1,133	$ 352	$ 575	$2,060	$1,140	$920	$3,840	24%
Strategy B	Selling Price per Unit	$12.00	$80.00	$54.00					
	Profit Contribution %	33.3	40	28	32				
	Expected volume-units	360	18	60					
	Sales	$4,320	$1,440	$3,240	$9,000				
	Profit contribution	1,440	576	840	2,856				
	Specific prog. and standby exp.	300	210	265	775				
		$1,140	$ 366	$ 575	$2,081	$1,340	$741	$3,840	19%

Exhibit 82

provide a means for reducing the forecasts and estimates made to a single evaluating factor which may be compared with alternative plans for investment. Some of the exhaustive analyses required for the return-on-investment computations lead to a more detailed collection of information, and therefore better decision making and more satisfactory results.

In our examination of techniques for computing return on investment for budgeting and planning, a number of considerations will not be covered. These include the consideration of risk or potential for success, intangible considerations which may be more important than financial ones, and the availability of funds to carry out all projects which may seem advantageous. There are also considerations after the fact which will not be given coverage here. One of these is the continuous review of plans and projects in light of long-range corporate goals; another is the desirability of and the necessity for postdecision review and follow-up to ascertain whether the return-on-investment objectives or expectations were, in fact, achieved as expected. Of course, the utilization of return-on-investment analysis for overall responsibility performance will tend to reflect the failure of responsible managers to attain objectives that affect overall performance.

The important elements of data necessary for computations of return on investment include the investment base for the computation and the costs and expected revenues which are related to the project evaluated. The concepts illustrated thus far are closely related to the so-called "book value" methods of computing the expected return on investment. While the book-value methods have serious limitations in evaluation, an examination of them will introduce more complex analyses and provide hypothetical models, which can be used to demonstrate return-on-investment calculations.

Book-value methods. A forecast of expected results is part of any project evaluation. The example given in Exhibit 83 describes the purchase of a piece of capital equipment, although the example could also reasonably apply to the investment in a new sales territory or a new product line. An initial investment of $10,000 is anticipated. The length of time for which the investment will be productive, that is, produce revenue for the company, is four years. The earnings of $1,000 annually might be from savings, added

sales, or another source. It has been assumed that the entire investment is subject to depreciation of $2,500 annually. In some cases
the total investment may not be of a type that can be depreciated
or amortized. The depreciation or amortization rate may not be
the same as the rate based on the economic life of the project.
These assumptions have been made for simplicity in illustration.

The return for this project on initial book value is computed in
Exhibit 83 by dividing the total book profit (profit *expected* to be
reflected on the annual profit-and-loss statement for the life of the
project) by the initial investment. This results in a return of 40
percent in cash flow. On an annual basis this amounts to 10 percent
(40 percent divided by 4 years).

Since the project returns the initial investment through profits
and the tax shield effect of depreciation, the actual investment
over the life of the project is not equal to the initial book value.
The initial investment of $10,000 is reduced to zero at the end of
the economic life of the project, and therefore we may say that
the average investment of $5,000 is a more appropriate base
for our return-on-investment calculation. This calculation is also
shown in Exhibit 83, and produces an annual return on investment
of 20 percent.

BOOK-VALUE METHODS OF ANALYSIS

Initial investment: $10,000

Economic life: 4 years
                           No salvage value

Return: $1,000 annually for 4 years
                           (after taxes and $2,500 depreciation
                           annually)

Method I: Return on Initial Book Value

$$\frac{\text{Book profit}}{\text{Initial book value}} = \frac{\$\ 4,000}{\$10,000} = 40\% \text{ total} = 10\% \text{ annually}$$

Method II: Return on Average Book Value

$$\frac{\text{Book profit}}{\text{Average book value}} = \frac{\$\ 4,000}{\$\ 5,000} = 80\% \text{ total} = 20\% \text{ annually}$$

Exhibit 83

While both of these methods are similar to the calculations used for evaluation of historical performance, they are invalid for projecting a return on investment where the investment precedes the time period expected for the planned receipt of revenue. For a project covering one to three years, the consequences of this may not be severe; however, in the evaluation of a research project covering five or eight years or a substantial investment in the introduction of a new product, the difference observed when taking into account the delay in receiving a return on the investment may make the difference between acceptance or rejection.

This is illustrated in Exhibit 84, where the hypothetical project—Project A—is compared with Project B, where all revenues are received in the fourth year. Each of these projects has a 10 percent return on initial book value and a 20 percent return on average book value. It is not necessary to dwell on the example to see that Project A, quickly returning cash for reinvestment in operations, is preferable to Project B, which will not provide a cash flow until the fourth year.

RETURN ON INITIAL BOOK VALUE

		After-Tax Profit on Project A	*After-Tax Profit on Project B*
Year	1	$1,000	$ 0
	2	1,000	0
	3	1,000	0
	4	1,000	4,000
	Total	$4,000	$4,000

Both projects have 10 percent return on initial book value and 20 percent return on average book value.

Exhibit 84

Payback method. Another familiar method utilized for evaluating investment opportunity is the so-called "payback" method. This is not actually a return-on-investment calculation, but rather a computation of the number of years required to recover the initial investment through savings, earnings, depreciation, or amortization. This evaluation is illustrated in Exhibit 85. The initial investment is divided by the cash flow generated by profit and depreciation to arrive at 2.9 years required to recover the initial investment of $10,000.

The technique shown in Exhibit 85 is often used to evaluate risk. One of the dangers of its use is illustrated in Exhibit 86. The cash flow generated by Project A, the hypothetical $10,000 project, is compared with Project C, with similar cash flows in the first three years of project life but a larger cash flow during the final year of project life. While both projects have 2.9-year paybacks,

PAYBACK METHOD OF ANALYSIS

The investment in Exhibit 83 is used here.

$$\frac{\text{Initial investment}}{\text{Cash flow per year}} = \text{Number of years to recover investment}$$

$$\frac{\$10,000}{\$1,000 \text{ profit} + \$2,500 \text{ depreciation}} = \frac{\$10,000}{\$ 3,500} = 2.9 \text{ years}$$

This method is a useful measure of risk, but not a measure of profitability.

Exhibit 85

RETURN USING PAYBACK METHOD

		Cash Flow on Project A	Cash Flow on Project C
Year	1	$ 3,500	$ 3,500
	2	3,500	3,500
	3	3,500	3,500
	4	3,500	5,500
	Total	$14,000	$16,000

Both projects show a 2.9-year payback period, but Project C is actually about one-third more profitable.

Exhibit 86

Project C will be preferable on a profitability basis even without the use of a more complex computational method. Again, in this calculation no consideration has been given to the fact that the cash flows in periods removed from the period of initial investment do not have the same economic value as the initial investment. These revenues are in effect tied up and may not be reinvested for alternative investment opportunities that may appear after the initial investment is committed to one of these projects.

Discounted cash flow. To compensate for the fact that revenues and investments often vary in amounts and apply to unrelated time periods, the techniques of discounted cash flow have been developed. The concepts of discounted cash flow relate to the fact that a dollar invested today at a certain rate of interest will increase in value as it remains invested, and this value will be compounded as the interest earned is added to the investment. As shown in the compound interest table in Exhibit 87, $1.00 invested at 10 percent in the first year will have a value of $1.10 at the end of the first year and a value of $1.61 at the end of the fifth year. On the other hand, the revenue dollar received at the end of the first year is worth less than a dollar received today, and a dollar received five years from today is of proportionately less value. Therefore, a dollar promised and received at the end of the first year has a value of only $0.91 today at an interest rate of 10 percent. A dollar received five years from today at 10 percent interest has a present value of $0.62; conversely, $0.62 invested today would be worth $1.00 in five years at 10 percent interest compounded annually.

Return-on-investment evaluation techniques are based upon this concept. Among them are the so-called "true rate of return" calculation, the excess present value method, and the annual excess value method. These three methods will be discussed briefly here. You may recognize these techniques and their modifications under other names in other publications.

True rate of return. To find the true rate of return, discount the cash flow generated by the project at a rate sufficient to result in the discounted cash inflow equaling the initial investment (cash outflow). Selection of the discount rate is a trial-and-error effort. Exhibit 88 illustrates this technique. A discount rate of 14 percent is tried initially. (The Present Worth Factors table in Exhibit 87 is used in these calculations.) The discounted cash flow totals $10,197.

TABLES OF COMPOUND INTEREST FACTORS

(Single Payment of One Dollar)

Compound Amount Factors $(1 + i)^N$

(The amount to which one dollar will grow if it earns i interest compounded for N periods.)

N	6%	8%	10%	12%	14%	16%	18%
0	1.000	1.000	1.000	1.000	1.000	1.000	1.000
1	1.060	1.080	1.100	1.120	1.140	1.160	1.180
2	1.124	1.166	1.210	1.254	1.300	1.346	1.392
3	1.191	1.260	1.331	1.405	1.482	1.561	1.643
4	1.262	1.360	1.464	1.574	1.689	1.811	1.939
5	1.338	1.469	1.611	1.762	2.925	2.100	2.288
6	1.419	1.587	1.772	1.974	2.195	2.436	2.700
7	1.504	1.714	1.949	2.211	2.502	2.826	3.185
20	3.207	4.661	6.727	9.646	13.743	19.461	27.393

Present Worth Factors $\dfrac{1}{(1 + i)^N}$

(The amount to which one dollar will grow by the end of N periods if it earns i interest compounded.)

N	6%	8%	10%	12%	14%	16%	18%
0	1.000	1.000	1.000	1.000	1.000	1.000	1.000
1	.943	.926	.909	.893	.877	.862	.847
2	.890	.857	.826	.797	.769	.743	.718
3	.840	.794	.751	.712	.675	.641	.609
4	.792	.735	.683	.636	.592	.552	.516
5	.747	.681	.621	.567	.519	.476	.437
6	.705	.630	.564	.507	.456	.410	.370
7	.665	.583	.513	.452	.400	.354	.314
20	.312	.215	.149	.104	.073	.051	.037

N = Number of compounding periods.

i = Interest rate per compounding period.

Exhibit 87

True Rate of Return
Discounted Cash Flow
On the Basis of Internal Rate of Return

Col. Year	1	2	3	4 (1 + 2 + 3)	5	6 (4 × 5)	7	8 (4 × 7)
	Expected Cash Flows				Expected Cash Flows Discounted			
		Profit after Depreciation and Taxes	Depreciation	Net Cash Flow	Discounted at 14%		Discounted at 16%	
	Investment				Factor	Amount	Factor	Amount
0	$(10,000)			$(10,000)	1.000	$(10,000)	1.000	$(10,000)
1	—	$1,000	$2,500	$ 3,500	.877	3,070	.862	3,017
2	—	1,000	2,500	3,500	.769	2,692	.743	2,601
3	—	1,000	2,500	3,500	.675	2,363	.641	2,244
4	—	1,000	2,500	3,500	.592	2,072	.552	1,932
		$4,000	$10,000	$ 14,000		$ 10,197		$ 9,793

Calculations—Valid and invalid

A	Discounted cash flow:	$14\% + \left(2\% \times \dfrac{(10,197 - 10,000)}{(10,197 - 9,794)}\right) = 15.0\%$	Valid
B	Return on initial book value:	$\dfrac{\$ 1,000}{\$10,000} = 10.0\%$	Invalid
C	Return on average book value:	$\dfrac{\$ 1,000}{\$ 5,000} = 20.0\%$	Invalid
D	Payback period:	$\dfrac{\$10,000}{\$ 3,500} = 2.9$ years	Conditionally useful

Exhibit 88

This amount is still greater than the initial investment, so a second trial is made, at 16 percent. A discounted sum of $9,793 is obtained using the factors at 16 percent. This sum is less than the initial investment of $10,000, and therefore we have placed the true annual rate of return in parentheses. Through interpolation the true rate of 15 percent is determined. Comparing these computations with the previous methods, we see that the true rate of return is higher than that obtained when we used the initial book value and lower than that obtained when the computation is based on the average book value. The true rate of return calculated by the discounted cash flow method portrays the average annual cash flow return on the investment remaining in the project (see Exhibit 89).

ANALYSIS OF DISCOUNTED CASH FLOW

Year	Investment (at Beginning of Year)	Total Cash Flow	Where Cash Flow Goes	
			Annual Earnings (15% of Investment)	Reduction of Investment
1	$10,000	$ 3,500	$1,500	$ 2,000
2	8,000	3,500	1,200	2,300
3	5,700	3,500	855	2,645
4	3,055	3,500	445*	3,055
5	0	X	X	X
Total	X	$14,000	$4,000	$10,000

*This figure has been rounded because the rate is not exactly 15 percent.

Exhibit 89

Excess present value. The true rate of return, while a valuable indication of the economic worth of a project, is difficult to relate directly to the other return-on-investment goals of the company and requires tedious repetition of the trial-and-error method to arrive at the correct discounted value. The excess present value method is a modification of the discounted cash flow procedure and is intended to overcome these two shortcomings.

Each segment of the firm is generally given a target or a minimum return expected as a contribution to corporate earnings. Specific projects are often given a higher rate of return target so that the overall corporate target may be achieved. This target for project return on investment is often called the "cutoff point." Using the cutoff point, we can simplify the discounted cash flow calculations. In Exhibit 90 a cutoff value of 10 percent for the present value has been used to evaluate the hypothetical illustration. All projects proposed by the same department would be evaluated using this same cutoff value. The net cash flow is extended by the present value at the minimum acceptable return on investment. Those projects which have a present value in excess of the investment have a rate of return greater than the acceptable cutoff. Those projects that have a present value less than the investment do not meet the criteria for return on investment.

In order to simplify the comparison of projects of different orders of magnitude, an excess present value index may be calculated by

EXCESS PRESENT VALUE METHOD OF ANALYSIS

Year	Net Cash Flow	Present Value Factors @ 10%	Present Value
0	$(10,000)	1.000	$(10,000)
1	$ 3,500	.909	$ 3,180
2	3,500	.826	2,890
3	3,500	.751	2,630
4	3,500	.683	2,390
Total	$ 14,000		$ 11,090
	Deduct initial investment		10,000
	Excess present value		$ 1,090

Refinement: Excess present value index method

$$\frac{\text{Sum of present values}}{\text{Initial investment}} = \frac{\$11,090}{\$10,000} = 1.1 \text{ Excess present value}$$

Exhibit 90

dividing the present value by the initial investment to achieve a ratio that is valid for comparison. Those projects with a ratio of less than 1.0 (a full return on the investment at the cutoff rate) do not meet the return-on-investment criteria of the department. Those projects exceeding a 1.0 ratio, at least, meet the return-on-investment requirements. A number of projects may be compared by ranking their present value indices.

Annual excess value. The annual excess value method treats each project as an annuity. The question is asked, "What will a certain investment today return in dollars over a specified period of time?" By using a set of annuity tables such as those illustrated in Exhibit 91, a factor can be selected that will represent the amount of equivalent annual cash flow required to return the expected rate of return or cutoff value. Applying this technique to the hypothetical project, a factor would be selected that over four annual periods would return the initial investment plus 10 percent. This factor, 0.315, when multiplied by the excess present value, as in Exhibit 92, gives an annual annuity of $345 after accounting for depreciation and return of 10 percent interest on the investment.

Return on investment represents a valuable tool for marketers. Where traditional techniques of measuring sales or advertising per-

TABLE OF ANNUITY FACTORS

(Amount per period to recover one dollar of investment.)

N	4%	6%	8%	10%	12%	14%	16%	18%
1	1.040	1.060	1.080	1.100	1.120	1.140	1.160	1.180
2	.530	.545	.560	.576	.592	.607	.623	.639
3	.360	.374	.388	.402	.416	.431	.445	.460
4	.275	.289	.302	.315	.329	.343	.357	.372
5	.225	.237	.250	.264	.277	.291	.305	.320
6	.191	.203	.216	.230	.243	.257	.271	.286
20	.074	.087	.102	.117	.134	.151	.169	.187

Exhibit 91

ANNUAL EXCESS VALUE

METHOD OF ANALYSIS

Year	Net Cash Flow	Present Value Factors @ 10%	Present Value
0	$(10,000)	1.000	$(10,000)
1	$ 3,500	.909	$ 3,180
2	3,500	.826	2,890
3	3,500	.751	2,630
4	3,500	.683	2,390
Total	$ 14,000		$ 11,090

Deduct initial investment   10,000

Excess present value $ 1,090

Excess present value $\times$ Annuity factor = Annual excess value

$$1,090 \times .3155 = \$345/\text{year}$$
$$(@ \ 10\%)$$

or

Annual net cash flow $3,500

Less annuity to amortize
investment and return
required company R.O.I. (10%)
    10,000 $\times$ .3155   3,155

    $ 345/year

Exhibit 92

formance, such as sales volume, have failed to relate to profit goals, return on investment succeeds. Where marketing measures have related poorly to financial and accounting records, return on investment requires better identification of marketing revenues, costs, and expenses, and provides better understanding of the interrelationships among marketing, finance, and profit goals. It is a measure that relates directly to the "bottom line" performance of a company.

Chapter XI

Controlling and Reporting
Marketing Costs

IN MANY COMPANIES plans are created, written, and filed
for management reference during the year. Often, because of daily
business pressures, the plan isn't formally referred to again until the
end of the year. At that time it is used as the basis of the next year's
plan. This is poor use of an important task. A plan should be the
mirror image of a company's control devices.

A company has many means of control. Management's observation of its employees is one form. Other controls include oral
reports, operating statistics, and formal written reports. In this
chapter the elements of formal reporting will be defined. These
are the controls that marketing management should use to make
sure that the business is proceeding according to plan.

It is clear that business must be planned to be effectively controlled. This can be observed by studying Exhibit 93. Merely to

SALES FORECAST ANALYSIS
(Sales for June: $157,243,552.98)
Westfield Stock Sales Company

Month	Sales (000's omitted)	Percent Under Forecast	Sales (000's omitted)	Percent Under Forecast
Jan.	$ 90	3%	$265	8%
Feb.	118	3	243	8
Mar.	126	4	225	7
Apr.	137	4	190	6
May	143	5	172	4
Jun.	157	6	157	2

Exhibit 93

show monthly sales in a report is meaningless. The *trend* of sales can be increasing or decreasing, under forecast or over forecast. While sales are *increasing* they can be *under* forecast, and while sales are *decreasing* they can be *over* forecast, depending upon the cyclical patterns involved. In other words, if control is to exist, an important control device must involve the relationship of actual results to plans or goals expressed in a way that makes the relationship evident to management so that corrective action can be taken.

In order to be meaningful, the reporting structure must be correlated with a company's planning. To report sales and not relate them to some level of expectation, even at the account level, becomes merely an exercise in which an interesting statistic is generated rather than a meaningful report.

ORGANIZATION AND CONTROL OF REPORTS

In order to be effective, reports must follow a firm's responsibility structure, portraying gradations of responsibility. A corporate statement of profits must be divisible into levels of geographic and product responsibilities. The geographic responsibility reports, in turn, must have levels by division, district, and territory. As in the

Badger Light Company case, top management should be able to isolate and explode performance in each layer.

The report structure must also portray the company in terms of its major areas of activity. In the product line reports of a consumer goods company, for example, it is impossible in one report to portray the performance of some 1,500 products. However, descriptions of these products often can be compressed into five to ten "businesses" that show the product lines to be planned and controlled.

EFFECTIVE REPORTING CONCEPTS

When a manager receives a performance report, he should be able to identify performance characteristics quickly, know if they are consistent with his plan, and be able to isolate those areas where management action is necessary. He should be able to call upon responsible persons to identify the reasons for the performances shown.

There are times when managers collate information from recent reports with data from previous reports. This is, essentially, a misuse of management time. Information should be so structured when presented to management that the report is self-contained. An example of such a report is shown in Exhibit 94. In this exhibit we see one module of a report containing:

1. Current information.
2. Quarterly summary information.
3. Planned volumes.
4. Variances.
5. Columnar totals to date.
6. The original forecast to date.
7. The yearly original forecast.
8. The current forecast (corrected and recast on the basis of experience to date).
9. Market indicator information such as share of market.
10. Incremental increase in market indicators since the last report.

This type of report module can be used in many reports. In Exhibits 95–99, the module concept of Exhibit 94 has been used.

THE SELF-CONTAINED REPORT CONCEPT

Unit of Measure

		Sales	
		Variance	*Actual/ Plan**
	Jan.	$ (3)	$ 90
	Feb.	(3)	118
	Mar.	(4)	126
	1st Quarter	(10)	334
	Apr.		141*
	May		148*
	Jun.		157*
Trend Format	2nd Quarter		
	Jul.		
	Aug.		
	Sep.		
	3rd Quarter		
	Oct.		
	Nov.		
	Dec.		
	Totals		$ 334

Statistical Area and Planned Position

	Variance	Actual/Plan
Original forecast to date		$ 344
Original forecast for year		$2,475
Current forecast	$(75)	$2,350
Market indicators		
Share		34%
Incremental share		+ 2%

*Planned results

Exhibit 94

STATEMENT OF NET EARNINGS, APRIL 1968
The Badger Light Company
(dollars in thousands)
Consolidated

( ) = Unfavorable variance   *Planned results

Year 1968	Gross Sales		Standard Profit Contribution on Gross Sales		Specific Product Line Expenses			Product Group Earnings		General Expenses				Operating Earnings Before taxes		Net Earnings	
	Var.	Actual/Plan*	Var.	Actual/Plan*	Variance	Actual	Prog'd. Plan	Var.	Actual/Plan*	Variance	Actual	Standby Plan	Prog'd. Plan	Var.	Actual/Plan*	Var.	Actual/Plan*
Jan.	149	2,850	52	970	(20)		145	32	825	(41)		195	420	(9)	210	(5)	109
Feb.	15	2,210	(12)	792	10		180	(2)	612	(6)		130	300	(8)	182	(4)	95
Mar.	(57)	2,550	(6)	946	(20)		180	(26)	766	12		170	400	(14)	196	(7)	102
1st Qtr.	107	7,610	34	2,708	(30)		505	4	2,203	(35)		495	1,120	(31)	588	(16)	306
Apr.	(75)	2,845*	(32)	1,042*	10		210	(42)	832*	10		160	400	(54)	262*	(27)	136*
May		2,600*		953*			200		753*			160	350		243*		126*
Jun.		2,753*		1,000*			210		790*			150	350		290*		151*
2nd Qtr.		8,123*		2,963*			630		2,333*			480	1,100		741*		386*
Jul.		2,110*		770*			200		570*			140	320		110*		57*
Aug.		1,980*		733*			190		543*			150	300		93*		48*
Sep.		1,614*		580*			175		405*			150	290		(35)*		(18)*
3rd Qtr.		5,704*		2,083*			565		1,518*			440	910		168*		87*
Oct.		2,335*		815*			200		615*			170	320		125*		65*
Nov.		2,995*		1,105*			220		885*			150	370		365*		190*
Dec.		3,440*		1,280*			210		1,070*			170	450		450*		233*
4th Qtr.		8,770*		3,200			630		2,570*			490	1,140		940*		488*
Year to date	182	10,455	66	3,750	(20)		715	46	3,035	(25)		655	1,530	21	850	11	442
Current plan		30,100		10,990			2,375		8,615			1,870	4,240		2,505		1,300
Original plan		29,500		10,920			2,300		8,620			1,870	4,280		2,470		1,283

Variance from Product Line Earnings

Product Line	Year to Date		
	Std. Profit Contribution	Direct Product Expenses	Product Line Earnings
Chandeliers	(11)	9	(2)
Spotlights	19	3	22
Close-to-wall	9	2	11
Outdoor fixtures	13	(3)	10
Circular recessed	11	(4)	7
Comm. spotlights	13	(7)	6
Rect. fluorescent	(3)	(14)	(17)
Comm. wall	21	(17)	4
Indus. fluorescent	8	(8)	2
Street lights	(14)	17	3
Total	66	(20)	46

Summary of Sales Division Variances

	Year to Date		
	Gross Sales	Standard Profit Contribution	Sales Division Expenses
Wholesale	(63)	(51)	(37)
Contract	245	115	11
Total	182	65	(26)

Summary of Expense Variances

	Current Month	Year to Date
VP of Manufacturing	23	6
VP of Sales	(11)	(26)
VP of Styling	3	5
VP of Personnel	(5)	(1)
VP of Merchandising	—	2
Exec. VP of Admin.	—	(11)
Total	10	(25)

Exhibit 95

Rectangular Fluorescent Fixtures Product Earnings
The Badger Light Company
April 1968
(000's omitted)

( ) = Unfavorable variance

*Planned results

Year 1967	Gross Sales		Standard Profit Contribution on Gross Sales				Specific Product Line Expenses		Product Line Earnings		Order Backlog	
			Percent		Amount							
	Var.	Actual/Plan*	Var.	Actual/Plan*	Var.	Actual/Plan*	Variances	Programmed	Var.	Actual/Plan*	Business Taken	Backlog
Jan.	100	1,240*	(2.0%)	35.3	13	438	(2)	70	11	368		
Feb.	10	1,394*	(1.1%)	37.1	(12)	517	—	19	(12)	498		
Mar.	(10)	883	0.5%	37.5	1	331	(8)	76	(7)	255		
1st Qtr.	100	3,517	(.1%)	36.6	2	1,286	(10)	165	(8)	1,121		
Apr.	(15)	1,234*	—	36.9*	(5)	455*	(4)	21*	(9)	434*		
May		1,231*		36.5*		450*		18*		432*		
Jun.		1,230*		36.6*		450*		16*		434*		
2nd Qtr.		3,710*		36.7*		1,360*		51*		1,309*		
Jul.		1,151*		37.3*		430*		18*		412*		
Aug.		1,060*		36.8*		390*		16*		374*		
Sep.		997*		37.1*		370*		18*		352*		
3rd Qtr.		3,208*		37.1*		1,190*		52*		1,138*		
Oct.		980*		36.8*		360*		18*		342*		
Nov.		945*		37.0*		350*		17*		333*		
Dec.		815*		36.8*		300*		18*		282*		
4th Qtr.		2,740*		36.9*		1,010*		53*		957*		

Year to Date	85	4,751	(0.8%)	36.6	(3)	1,741	(14)	186	(17)	1,555
Current plan		13,110			36		4,721		303		4,418
Original plan		13,075			37		4,844		311		4,533

Summary of Variance from Profit Plan

	Planned Product Group Earnings	Standard Profit Contribution		Product Group Expenses				Actual Product Group Earnings
		Volume	Mix	Adv. Pub.	Mark-downs	Cost of Returns	Catalogs	
Month	443	(5)	—	(2)	4	(5)	(1)	434
Year to date	1,572	31	(34)	(6)	7	(10)	(5)	1,555

Exhibit 96

WHOLESALE SALES DIVISION EARNINGS
The Badger Light Company
April 1968
(000's omitted)

( ) = Unfavorable variance

*Planned results

Year 1967	Gross Sales		Standard Profit Contribution on Gross Sales		Specific Sales Division Expenses		Division Earnings	
	Var.	Actual/Plan*	Var.	Actual/Plan*	Variance Actual	Standby and Prog'd. Plan	Var.	Actual/Plan*
Jan.	(47)	2,107	(40)	823	(11)	183	(51)	640
Feb.	(51)	2,213	(43)	829	(21)	194	(61)	635
Mar.	10	1,997	12	757	(5)	156	7	601
1st Qtr.	(88)	6,317	(71)	2,409	(37)	533	(108)	1,876
Apr.	25	1,875*	21	703*	—	204	21	499*
May		2,110*		760*		205		555*
Jun.		2,048*		699*		212		487*
2nd Qtr.		6,008*		2,162*		621		1,541*
Jul.		1,752*		682*		190		492*
Aug.		1,310*		508*		160		348*
Sep.		983*		370*		150		220*
3rd Qtr.		4,045*		1,560*		500		1,060*
Oct.		1,566*		603*		170		433*
Nov.		2,722*		1,047*		200		847*
Dec.		2,714*		1,044*		240		804*
4th Qtr.		7,002*		2,694*		610		2,084*
Year to date	(63)	8,192	(50)	3,112	(37)	737	(87)	2,375

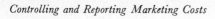

	Current plan	Original plan
	23,460	24,030
	8,896	9,140
	2,264	2,420
	6,632	6,720

Summary of Territorial Variances
Year to Date

	Gross Sales	*Standard Profit Contribution*	*Territorial Expenses*	*Territorial Earnings*
New England	—	(1)	—	(1)
Met. New York	10	3	(2)	1
Mid Atl.	(44)	(37)	(21)	(58)
South	5	4	2	6
Met. Chicago	5	1	(2)	(1)
Midwest	1	(4)	5	1
Southwest	(7)	1	—	1
West	(33)	(17)	10	(7)
General			(29)	(29)
Total division	(63)	(50)	(37)	(87)

Exhibit 97

MIDDLE ATLANTIC TERRITORY EARNINGS
The Badger Light Company
April 1968
(000's omitted)

( ) = Unfavorable variance   *Planned results

Year 1967	Gross Sales		Standard Profit Contribution		Specific Territorial Exp.		Territorial Earnings	
					Variance	Standby and Programmed		
	Var.	Actual/Plan*	Var.	Actual/Plan*	Actual	Plan	Var.	Actual/Plan*
Jan.	(13)	440	(4)	163	(19)	41	(23)	122
Feb.	(4)	420	(4)	158	(1)	23	(5)	135
Mar.	(18)	370	(15)	129	(1)	23	(16)	106
1st Qtr.	(35)	1,230	(23)	450	(21)	87	(44)	363
Apr.	(9)	393	(14)	147	—	20	(14)	127
May		406*		155*		19		136*
Jun.		403*		158*		18		140*
2nd Qtr.		1,211*		474*		57		417*
Jul.		400*		150*		16		134*
Aug.		349*		126*		16		110*
Sep.		355*		131*		16		115*
3rd Qtr.		1,104*		407*		48		359*
Oct.		343*		130*		12		118*
Nov.		320*		122*		11		111*
Dec.		227*		84*		11		73*
4th Qtr.		890*		336*		34		302*

Year to date	(44)	1,623	(57)	597	(21)	107	(58)	490

Current plan	4,550	1,730	215	1,515
Original plan	4,470	1,690	205	1,485

	Planned Territory Earnings	Standard Profit Contribution		Territorial Expenses				Actual Territory Earnings
		Volume	Price and Mix	Selling Compensation	Selling (Adv-Prom)	Selling (Other)	Admin.	
Year to date	548	(17)	(20)	(6)	(8)	(2)	(5)	490

Summary of Salesman Variances

Salesman	Current Month Standard Profit Contribution
Abner	(13.8)
Barber	2.0
Dolan	6.4
Johns	5.1
Majur	(0.1)
Nelson	10.0
Toms	(1.5)
Vinon	(0.5)
General Variance	(11.6)
Total for Territory	(14)

Exhibit 98

SALESMAN'S PERFORMANCE ANALYSIS
The Badger Light Company
(000's omitted)

Salesman: Abner   Month: April

( ) = Unfavorable variance

Week	Sales % Ful.	Sales Act.	Profit Contribution $ Var.	Profit Contribution $ Act.	Profit Contribution % Var.	Profit Contribution % Act.
4–7	75	12.5	(2.4)	3.1	(8.0)	24.8
4–14	90	11.5	(2.6)	4.0	(6.0)	34.8
4–21	81	10.0	(3.3)	3.2	(6.0)	32.0
4–28	54	6.1	(5.5)	2.3	(8.3)	37.7
Total April	74	40.1	(13.8)	12.6	(7.0)	31.5

Call Analysis

	Calls Var.	Calls Act.	Sales/Call Var.	Sales/Call Act.	No. New Cust. Var.	No. New Cust. Act.
4–7	(2)	20	(.13)	.63	(4)	—
4–14	(4)	18	(.10)	.64	(5)	—
4–21	(3)	20	(.27)	.50	1	3
4–28	(8)	19	(.31)	.32	(6)	—
Total April	(17)	77	(.20)	.52	(14)	3

Order Analysis

	Orders Var.	Orders Act.	Sales/Order Var.	Sales/Order Act.	Multi-Prod. as % of Total Var.	Multi-Prod. as % of Total Act.	Special Order Var.	Special Order Act.
4–7	(1)	15	(.17)	.83	5.3	85.3	(4)	7
4–14	(5)	12	—	.96	(2.9)	78.1	(5)	10
4–21	5	19	(.74)	.53	(8.6)	71.4	(9)	14
4–28	(4)	14	(.50)	.44	(8.0)	72.0	1	4
Total April	(5)	60	(.37)	.67	(3.8)	76.2	(17)	35

Remarks:

Ill April 26.

Exhibit 99

This application ranges from the corporate statement of net earnings into the marketing area and down to the salesman's performance analysis.

Information can also be shown graphically, as in Exhibit 100, which shows the Standwell Construction Company's accumulated profit contribution for five months and the target for the year. Graphic presentation, at the product line or at the responsibility level of reporting, is an excellent means of calling attention to current performance and presenting projections. With the advent of computer graphics, this type of report is being produced by computer in some companies.

A New Jersey-based major industrial company produces a graphic lead sheet as the first page of the monthly reports for each division within the firm. The company shows the four or five key indicators of the division's performance, such as sales, equipment utilization, manpower utilization, and profit contribution. Management has grown so accustomed to the graphic portrayal that it insists on its appearance in the monthly report.

Frequency of reports and distribution. In almost all companies there is continual discussion regarding information distribution. Firms usually tend to restrict the circulation of information. Information distribution should be tied to the responsibility structure of the company. If a manager is able to influence cost or revenue, he should see the resulting plans and reports. If information is controllable in a monthly cycle (as in the case of sales or commissions), it should be reported on a monthly cycle. If it is not that sensitive, perhaps quarterly reporting would suffice. An example of this is the report of assets managed (ROAM) in a sales division. A monthly report was generated in a company where the reporting of assets managed was included as a measure of a manager's performance. It was apparent that the manager could neither react to nor influence this measure in his daily operations, but the indicator was responsive to his longer-range planning. The ROAM indicator was then produced on a quarterly basis, and management reaction and review were geared to the quarterly period.

In some cases a daily report is necessary. A flash report, such as for flash sales, is often used, and it is often related to a meaningful indicator such as passenger mile or seat utilization in the airline industry. These reports are meaningful in situations where mer-

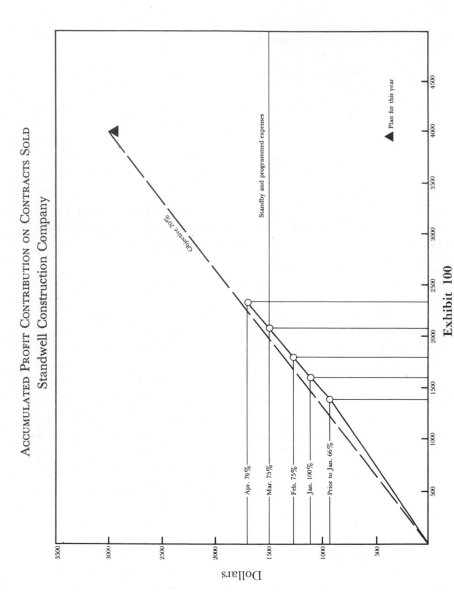

ACCUMULATED PROFIT CONTRIBUTION ON CONTRACTS SOLD
Standwell Construction Company

Exhibit 100

chandise is perishable, and management reaction must be geared to the rapid disposition of a commodity (such as a vacant passenger seat) on a daily cycle.

Exception reporting. Improved control can be achieved when management can concentrate on situations which are exceptions to a plan. This allows management to concentrate on the creative operation of a business, rather than on the drudgery of interpreting too much information. In a report structure such as that portrayed for the Badger Light Company in Exhibits 95–99, reports can be automated and exception reports generated. With the advent of the computer and automated technology, upper and lower control limits and parameters can be programmed into the computer. Reports are able to be structured so that exception situations are highlighted, or flash exception reports generated when the control limits are exceeded by more than an acceptable deviation. An example of an exception report would be a report to the product manager that his product line is selling at a rate more than 5 percent behind planned sales during a particular month.

An exception report generated during a month permits management reaction during a report period. Rather than reacting from a historical report several days after the end of the month, management can act closer to "real time." A reporting system geared to produce exception reports becomes a tool for management rather than just a scorecard.

The control process generates information for management during a planning cycle. Formal controls are generally reports. Reports should be readable, concise, and fully integrated. A fully integrated report does not require reference to other reports or plans to be meaningful and occupies a definite position within the layers of reports in a firm. A viable reporting system is tailored to management's concept of how its business and functions are organized.

Chapter XII

An Integrated Marketing/Financial
Information System

IN HIS BOOK *The American Challenge*, J.-J. Servan-Schrei-ber details many of the factors that have made American business concepts successful. In his concluding chapter, describing these reasons for America's greatness, Servan-Schreiber indicates that underlying the drive and ability to mobilize technology, American economic force has become great because "Its weapons are the use and systematic perfection of all the instruments of reason. Not simply in the field of science, where it is the only tool, but also in organization and management . . . ." The organization of information within a company into a viable structure of reports, and into an information system, is one of the modern tools of planning and control that assists American management in implementing its market-oriented production techniques.

In this book we have explained some of the concepts inherent in a marketing information system. In order to be effective, that system must combine not only marketplace information but the data within the financial information system. The intent of an integrated marketing/financial information system is to express market conditions in terms relating to financial performance. This requires assembling financial information on a basis that conforms to the marketing data used by each level of marketing management. In addition it requires expressing these data in formats that conform to the responsibility structure of the organization.

In the case of the Badger Light Company, the marketing information system was designed for what many marketers would consider to be an industrially oriented company. In this chapter we will portray the information system in the National Cookie Company, a pseudonym for an existing consumer products concern.

THE NATIONAL COOKIE COMPANY: ORGANIZATIONAL STRUCTURE

The National Cookie Company is a large manufacturer of baked products, and has worldwide production and marketing facilities. The organizational structure of the United States group is shown in Exhibit 101. The company uses product managers because of the individual attention they are able to give to the major product lines. Their major responsibility is to integrate the planning and marketing effort of their products into the company's overall product and market plan. As in many other consumer goods companies, all the products are handled by a single sales force.

The company's annual advertising, sales promotion, and market research expense is in excess of $45 million. This is approximately 17.5 percent of sales dollars and nearly three times the contemplated net profit of the corporation. Experience has shown that sales of the firm's products are quite sensitive to advertising. Accordingly, effective measures in this area are vital to meaningful management decision making.

The company has five large competitors, all having approximately equal financial resources. In addition, there are many small bakeries in the market areas served by the company. These bakeries share the market significantly in their local areas, but do not constitute a major threat to the National Cookie Company.

ORGANIZATION CHART

The National Cookie Company

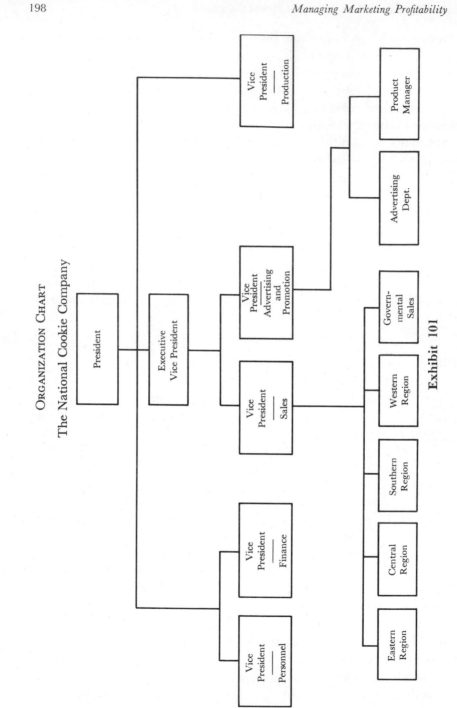

Exhibit 101

Description of Financial Reporting Statements

The National Cookie Company recently redesigned its statement of earnings form. It did this in order to provide better readability and to correspond with the marketer's concept of corporate operations (see Exhibit 102). The statement is prepared so that a "plateau" of earnings—the product line earnings—is shown, which identifies the direct product line revenues produced by each business segment (product line) minus the expenses directly associated with these revenues. This plateau provides top management with a clear focus for measuring the effectiveness of the people responsible for product line performance. In effect, the product line earnings plateau forms a cutoff in management's mind for the marketing responsibility area. All expenses to the right of product line earnings in Exhibit 102 are not necessarily associated with marketing performance. The columns to the left of product line earnings are influenced by revenue and by expenses within the marketing areas of decision making. The display of variances from product line earnings shown on the statement of earnings permits top management identification of differences between actual and planned earnings in each of the business segments.

While the statement of earnings is now oriented to marketing needs, it is also an integrated control tool for measuring nonmarketing departmental performance. A summary of expense variances is displayed on the statement of earnings. These are the functional or nonproduct line variances, the other necessary expense "cut" that permits quick identification of off-target expense performance within the organizational segment responsible for that performance.

Top management, seeing both product line earning variances and functional expense variances, can plan and control the areas of manufacturing, distribution, selling, and general administration, and look to the product line manager to explain good or poor product line performance.

The Product Manager's Reports

At the National Cookie Company each product manager receives a product line statement of earnings that ties into the

STATEMENTS OF EARNINGS
The National Cookie Company
(000's omitted)

( ) = Unfavorable variance

* Planned results
Dollars in thousands

Date 1968	Net Sales Var.	Net Sales Actual/Plan*	Standard Profit Contribution on Net Sales Var.	Standard Profit Contribution Actual/Plan*	Cost of Returns Actual/Plan*	Adv. S. Prom & Mkt. Res. Surveys Actual/Plan*	Fixed Mfg. Plan	Product Line Earnings Var.	Product Line Earnings Actual/Plan*	Allocated Indirect Expenses Plan	Expense Variance Actual	Operating Profit Var.	Operating Profit Actual/Plan*	Other Income & Ded. Actual/Plan*	Taxes Actual/Plan*	Net Profit Var.	Net Profit Actual/Plan*
Jan.	(1,496)	35,782	94	18,116	44	5,376	1,530	72	11,166	3,802	204	276	7,568	(8)	4,024	298	3,536
Feb.	(3,242)	19,022	(2,046)	9,628	48	3,718	1,174	(2,138)	4,688	2,632	124	(1,014)	2,180	12	1,166	(380)	1,026
Mar.	6,230	34,258	2,988	17,454	84	5,346	1,164	1,146	10,860	3,344	540	2,686	8,056	122	4,350	1,434	3,828
1st Qtr.	1,492	89,062	1,036	45,198	176	14,440	3,868	1,080	26,714	9,778	868	1,948	17,804	126	9,540	1,352	8,390
Apr. May Jun.																	
2nd Qtr.		68,650*		35,116*	420*	11,546*	3,816		19,334*	8,818			10,516*	(112)*	5,704*		4,700*
Jul. Aug. Sep.																	
3rd Qtr.		58,108*		28,262*	238*	9,864*	3,882		15,278*	8,342			6,936*	(216)*	3,684*		3,036*
Oct. Nov. Dec.																	
4th Qtr.		51,204*		24,984*	216*	9,614*	3,886		11,268*	8,482			2,786*	(364)*	1,328*		1,094*
Year to date	1,492	89,062	1,036	45,198	176	14,440	3,868	1,080	26,714	9,778	868	1,948	17,804	126	9,540	1,352	8,390
Current plan		265,532		133,524	1,342	45,216	15,452		71,514	35,420			36,094	(970)	19,256		15,868

Variances from Product Line Earnings

	Year to Date			
	Std. Profit Contrib.	Loss on Returns	Adv. Prom. Mkt. Res.	Prod. Line Earnings
Bread	548	8	72	628
Snacks	142	(2)	(774)	(92)
Cookies	(142)	136	284	278
Crackers	216	78	62	356
Pretzels	(14)	—	24	10
Cereals	(72)	—	62	(10)
Frozen	(120)	—	—	(120)
Dairy	(38)	—	2	(36)
Cakes	(25)	72	20	66
Total	1,035	292	(248)	1,080

Summary of Expense Variances

	Year to Date	Current Month
Manufacturing Incurred	874	
Expenses	64	72
Distribution	346	240
Adv. and Sales Prom. Dept.	62	(42)
Mkt. Research Dept.	—	(8)
Personnel	68	68
Technical Research Dept.	24	24
Sales Depts.	4	4
General Admin. Depts.	76	78
Inventory Re-evaluation	224	4
Total	868	540

Exhibit 102

STATEMENT OF EARNINGS, COOKIE LINE
The National Cookie Company

( ) = Unfavorable variance

* Planned results

Dollars in thousands

Date 1968	Sales						Standard Profit Contribution on Net Sales			Direct Product Expenses					Product Line Earnings	
	Net Units		Gross	Net Dollars						Adv.	Sales Prom.	Mkt. Res.	Cost of Re-turns	Fixed Man.		
	Var.	Actual	Actual	Actual/Plan*	Var.	Var.	Actual/Plan*	Sales %		Actual/Plan*	Actual/Plan*	Act./Plan*	Act./Plan*	Actual/Plan*	Var.	Actual/Plan*
Jan.	28	798	4,573	4,528	138	165	2,328	51.4		668	294	22	24	286		1,034
Feb.	(140)	560	3,665	3,630	(964)	(515)	1,856	51.1		564	322	14	26	230		700
Mar.	76	626	4,848	4,712	442	208	2,418	51.3		584	436	18	40	230	330	1,110
1st Qtr.	(36)	1,984	13,086	12,870	(384)	(142)	6,602	51.3		1,816	1,052	54	90	746	278	2,844
Apr. May Jun.																
2nd Qtr.				7,192*			3,702*	50.1*		594*	136*	64*	252*	748*		1,908*
Jul. Aug. Sep.																
3rd Qtr.				11,084*			5,566*	50.2*		842*	794*	80*	166*	748*		2,936*

Oct.												
Nov.												
Dec.												
4th Qtr.	15,396*			7,778*	49.9*	2,492*	972*	80*	148*	748*		3,338*
Year to Date	12,870	(384)	(142)	6,602	51.3	1,816	1,052	54	90	746	278	2,844
Current plan	47,126			23,790		6,070	2,900	290	792	2,990		10,748

(Oct.: (36); Nov.: 1,984, 13,086)

Standard Profit Contribution Variance

	YTD	This Month
Volume	(120)	258
Sales mix	(22)	(50)
Total	(142)	208

Net Product Line Earnings Variance

	YTD	This Month
Standard profit contribution var.	(142)	208
Advertising variance	326	174
Sales promotion variance	(54)	(104)
Purchased market research var.	12	2
Cost of returns variance	136	50
Total	278	330

Exhibit 103

corporate statement of earnings relating directly to his product line. An example of this is shown in Exhibit 103, which details the factors accounting for the profit performance of the firm's cookie line. Some of the control highlights in this statement include identification of the following:

- Standard profit contribution. By using a standard profit contribution, the cookie line is isolated from possible off-pace variances of other functional departments or product lines. Standard profit contribution represents sales minus *standard* incremental, distribution, and manufacturing expenses.
- Direct product expenses. These reduce standard profit contribution to product line earnings. Advertising, promotion, market research, cost of returns, and fixed manufacturing costs are shown as direct product expenses.
- Product line profit contribution. The contribution of product line earnings of this product line to corporate profits. In effect this is the product line earnings plateau.

The product line earnings statement identifies the portion of the revenue and profit for which each product manager is responsible. This statement is essentially a financial one, but it also shows the volume and sales mix the manager can work to control. The statement does not indicate markets where profit opportunities exist, competitive conditions, or changes in the marketplace. Market research supplies management with a documentation of some of these conditions, but the relationship between this information and profits is not always clear.

In many companies product managers must improvise or devise "off-line" systems to portray the relationship between profitability and market research data. The tools for the manager to tune his products' performance to the market should be part of the integrated marketing/financial information system.

It is the product manager's job to increase the total share of the market and to maximize profits. Often ignored is the fact that for many products, in certain markets, there is a smaller, more profitable market share. One function of an integrated marketing/financial information system is the expression of market conditions in terms of their relationship to profit performance. This requires assembling financial information on a basis that conforms to the market research data used by each level of marketing management. The information system should portray the realities of relationships as they interact to produce market performance, and thereby identify areas of opportunity or areas of profit versus market share tradeoffs.

Marketing management requires specially designed reports to integrate marketing and financial information. Examples of these nonfinancial, but integrated, reports follow.

Financial and marketing information summary by consumer product lines (see Exhibit 104). This report provides marketing management with a "best" estimate of the profit and marketing expenses to compare with market research information normally received. For example, when Exhibit 104 was analyzed, the data disclosed certain relevant facts:

- The extent to which each line "carried" or "was carried by" others. This is obtained by the comparison of the percent of gross standard profit contribution and the percent of advertising and sales promotion. As an example, the bread product line contributed 59 percent of gross standard profit contribution and absorbed only 40 percent of the total advertising and sales promotion dollar.
- The "cost" or "opportunity rate" associated with spending decisions. This is shown by the display of gross standard profit contribution per dollar of expenses for advertising and sales promotion. In the bread line, $4.94 of gross standard profit contribution was received for each advertising and sales promotion dollar spent on the line.
- The profits for each line. These are shown as net product line earnings, obtained by subtracting from the gross standard profit contribution the direct product expenses that were incurred in producing those profits. In the bread line, with a gross standard profit contribution of $26,230, there were $7,300 of total direct product line expenses. Product line earnings are $18,930.
- The size of the market in which the spending took place. In the bread line, a specialty market, it was estimated that total market sales equaled $63,862,000. Our sales of

FINANCIAL AND MARKETING INFORMATION SUMMARY FOR CONSUMER PRODUCT LINES

The National Cookie Company

(000's omitted)

	Total	Bread	Snacks	Cookies	Crackers	Pretzels	Cereals
Gross sales volume							
Equivalent units	—	28,808	1,126	2,014	3,042	2	6
Dollar sales	$86,886	$53,450	$ 9,966	$13,086	$10,334	$ 10	$ 40
Gross standard profit cont.	$44,334	$26,230	$ 5,782	$ 6,602	$ 5,698	$ 6	$ 16
Direct expenses							
Advertising	$ 4,722	$ 1,550	$ 718	$ 1,764	$ 670	$ (2)	$ 22
Sales promotion	8,868	3,716	3,032	1,052	1,054	—	12
Production of adv. and sales prom.	200	40	6	52	98	—	4
Loss on returns	500	122	150	90	126	10	2
Purchased market research	278	48	54	54	62	—	60
Budgeted fixed manufacturing	3,602	1,824	522	746	394	112	04
Total direct expenses	18,170	7,300	4,484	3,758	2,404	120	104
Net product line earnings	$26,164	$18,930	$ 1,298	$ 2,844	$ 3,294	$(114)	$(88)
Analysis							
Percent total G.S.P.C.*; Percent A. & P.†	00%;100%	59%;40%	13%;27%	15%;20%	13%;13%		
Profit opportunity rate							
this quarter	3.21	4.94	1.54	2.30	3.13		
last quarter	3.05	5.01	2.25	2.25	2.95		
Total dollar market							
this quarter		$63,862	$10,068	$25,142	$28,652		
last quarter		64,624	10,170	26,790	27,664		
Share of market							
this quarter		83%	99%	61%	37%		
last quarter		84%	98%	60%	37%		
Percent distribution		98%	97%	95%	94%		

*G.S.P.C. = Gross Standard Profit Contribution.
†A. & P. = Advertising and Promotion.

Exhibit 104

$53,450,000 of these specialty breads amounted to 83 percent of the market.

- The market penetration. This is shown in the percent distribution figure, which indicates that the bread product line is available in 98 percent of the stores that constitute this specialty bread market.

Financial and marketing information summary—cookie line by variety. A product manager is usually responsible for a line which includes a number of distinct products as well as varieties within a product line. These products typically sell at different prices and yield different percentages of profit contribution. The product manager must weigh the unit profitability and the responsiveness of volume to marketing effort for each variety to determine an optimum allocation of effort among the product varieties. The variety operating statement, shown in Exhibit 105, reports the revenues produced by each variety, and the expenses assigned to each variety. Standard profit contribution in the variety operating statement is computed on the basis of gross sales rather than net sales.

Determining the gross standard profit contribution for each variety presents no problem. Accurately assigning variety marketing cost, however, is complicated by the fact that the sales force sells all products in the line. Also, it is difficult to distinguish among advertising for the company's brands of cookies that differ only in flavor or shape. While it is true that all the varieties in the line benefit from the commercials or other promotions which feature one of the varieties, it is misleading to allocate the costs of those promotions to all product varieties. In this report, marketing efforts are charged to the *featured* product, variety, or varieties in any one advertisement.

The variety contribution to a product line's profits is referred to as the gross product line earnings. Advertising and promotional efforts which feature all varieties are classified as direct line expenses and are not allocated to individual varieties. Unit costs are portrayed at the gross standard profit contribution level; variety expenses which are programmed expenses are portrayed at the gross product line earnings level. Direct line expenses, such as some fixed manufacturing expense, and market research cannot be assigned to any of the varieties. These expenses reduce the gross

FINANCIAL AND MARKETING INFORMATION SUMMARY
The National Cookie Company
Cookie Product Line, by Variety

Dollars in thousands

	Total	Oatmeal		Chocolate	Butterscotch		Peanut Butter
		96's	48's		48's	48's	48's
Gross sales volume							
Equivalent units	2,014	844		80	426		88
Dollar sales	$13,086	$4,836		$556	$3,014		$600
Selling price	$ 6,378	$5.67	$5.57	$6.90	$6.90	$6.90	$6.90
Variable mfg. and dist. at stnd.		$2.57	$2.58	$3.54	$3.40	$3.47	$3.84
Standard profit cont. per unit		$3.10	$3.17	$3.36	$3.50	$3.43	$3.06
%		54.7	55.1	48.7	50.7	49.7	44.3
Gross standard profit cont.	$ 6,602	$2,558		$274	$1,486		$266
Direct variety expenses							
Variety advertising	$ 1,406	$ 558		$ 8	$ 18		$130
Variety sales promotion	958	436		30	216		36
Prod. of variety adv. and sales prom.	38	18		—	2		2
Loss on returns	90	18		8	8		16
Gross product line earnings	$ 4,110	$1,634		$228	$1,242		$ 82
Direct line expenses							
Line adv. and sales prom. and production	$ 466						
Purchased market research	54						
Budgeted fixed manufacturing	746						
Total direct line expenses	1,266						
Net product line earnings	$ 2,844						
Analysis							
% line G.S.P.C.; % of variety A. & P.	100; 100	39	42	4	23	10	4
Opportunity rate	2.75	2.53		7.21	6.30		1.58
L.O.R.* per $ variety adv. and sales prom.	.37	.02		.21	.03		.10
	2.38	2.51		7.00	6.27		1.48
Market data							
Total $ market size (this qtr.-last qtr.)	$25,142–$26,790						
Variety distribution % Apr.-Feb.	95 95	86	87	55 56	93	93	61 61

*L.O.R. = Loss on Returns.

(Continued)

Dollars in thousands

	Nuts	Sugar	Vanilla	Marshmallow	Cocoanut
Gross sales volume					
Equivalent units	76	20	88	218	80
Dollar sales	$522	$144	$654	$1,596	$586
Selling price	$ 6.90	$ 6.90	$ 7.35	$ 7.35	$ 7.35
Variable mfg. and dist. at stnd.	$ 3.48	$ 3.30	$ 3.92	$ 3.70	$ 3.72
Standard profit cont. per unit	$ 3.42	$ 3.60	$ 3.43	$ 3.65	$ 3.63
%	49.6	52.2	46.7	49.7	49.4
Gross standard profit cont.	$268	$ 76	$302	$ 812	$288
Direct variety expenses					
Variety advertising	$ 8	$ 8	$152	$ 374	$130
Variety sales promotion	28	6	36	110	30
Prod. of variety adv. and sales prom.	—	—	4	8	4
Loss on returns	18	34	18	6	4
Gross product line earnings	$214	$ 28	$ 92	$ 314	$120
Direct line expenses					
Line adv. and sales prom. and production					
Purchased market research					
Budgeted fixed manufacturing					
Total direct line expenses					
Net product line earnings					
Analysis					
% line G.S.P.C.; % of variety A. & P.	4	1	5	12	4
Opportunity rate	7.44	5.43	1.57	1.65	1.76
L.O.R. per $ variety adv. and sales prom.	.50	2.43	.09	.01	.02
	6.94	3.00	1.48	1.64	1.74
Market data					
Total $ market size (this qtr.-last qtr.)	58	30	54	67	60
Variety distribution % Apr.-Feb.	59	30	54	65	60

Exhibit 105

product line earnings to a net product line earnings figure (see Exhibit 105). This figure ($2,844,000) corresponds with that given in the consumer product lines summary in Exhibit 104.

The financial and marketing information summary by product line, as exhibited in the cookie product line statement, shows the extent to which each variety of cookies is "carrying" or "being carried by" the line. For example, the oatmeal cookie is being carried to the extent that it constitutes 39 percent of the product line G.S.P.C., but absorbs 42 percent of the line's advertising and promotion dollar. The opportunity rates associated with decisions and the market trends and competitive activity within the period are also shown.

This statement allows the product manager to see both the financial results of his product lines and the results of his marketing efforts directly related to those financial results. It is a marketing decision-oriented performance reporting system.

Cookie product line variety profitability by sales region. The United States is not one market, but a number of distinct marketing centers. These markets react differently to applications of advertising, sales promotion, and marketing dollars. Products react differently within these markets. Often, the decisions about the weight and form of marketing effort are made on the basis of net wholesale units or estimated retail units sold in each area. If this is to be changed from a unit share concept to a profit maximization concept, then profits and deductions from profits must be reported by the sales region or territory, and by varieties within regions. Specifically, the financial function must supply product management with the gross standard profit contribution, the variety advertising and sales promotion expenses which produced it, and the effect of loss on returns by variety, by market. This presents a problem of data digestion for the manager. In order for him to understand and quickly assimilate the data supplied, an index which relates the relevant variables is needed. This index is the previously mentioned *profit opportunity rate*, which is the gross standard profit contribution per dollar of direct advertising and promotion.

The cookie product line variety profitability by sales region report (Exhibit 106) includes the total *dollars* of gross standard profit contribution and the profit opportunity rate. The latter rate does not show areas of limited potential or marginal markets; al-

COOKIE PRODUCT LINE VARIETY PROFITABILITY BY SALES REGION
The National Cookie Company

*1 Profit opportunity rate—gross standard profit contribution per dollar of direct advertising and promotion
*2 Total gross standard profit contribution dollars

	Rank	Total Cookie Product Line *1 Per $	*2 Total	Oatmeal Per $	Total	Butterscotch Per $	Total	Marshmallow Per $	Total	Vanilla Per $	Total	Peanut Butter Per $	Total	Cocoanut Per $	Total	Chocolate Per $	Total	Nut Per $	Total
Eastern Region																			
Territory 1	5	$3.17	$ 698	$3.30	$ 254	$ 6.00	$ 156	$ 2.50	$ 94	$2.90	$ 46	$2.80	$ 34	$ 2.80	$ 34	$10.50	$ 42	$ 4.20	$ 28
Territory 2	11	2.54	1,358	2.63	756	5.30	180	1.10	152	1.70	80	1.00	42	1.20	42	8.00	46	6.00	58
Territory 3	6	3.07	644	2.30	248	5.70	138	1.40	84	1.60	36	1.10	24	1.00	22	5.30	28	13.00	26
Territory 4	8	2.69	580	3.30	282	6.00	72	2.30	86	1.60	26	1.60	26	2.60	26	5.50	22	9.00	18
Total		$2.75	$3,290	$2.71	$1,540	$ 5.70	$ 546	$ 1.50	$415	$1.80	$188	$1.40	$126	$ 1.50	$132	$ 7.10	$128	$ 6.70	$120
Central Region																			
Territory 5	13	$2.31	$ 448	$2.50	$ 170	$ 5.50	$ 130	$ 1.90	$ 53	$ .60	$ 8	$1.70	$ 10	$ 2.20	$ 22	$ 3.50	$ 14	$ 6.00	$ 12
Territory 6	12	2.33	466	2.60	172	5.80	122	1.60	55	1.10	16	1.70	20	2.30	28	2.50	10	—	26
Territory 7	14	2.23	178	2.10	54	4.20	42	2.40	24	3.00	6	2.50	10	2.00	8	5.00	10	—	8
Territory 8	15	2.04	188	1.90	58	5.50	52	1.50	24	.70	4	1.35	8	1.30	8	5.00	10	—	6
Total		$2.25	$1,280	$2.40	$ 454	$ 6.20	$ 346	$ 1.80	$162	$ .90	$ 34	$1.60	$ 48	$ 2.10	$ 66	$ 3.70	$ 44	$26.00	$ 52
Southern Region																			
Territory 9	7	$2.94	$ 94	$2.00	$ 20	$ 6.00	$ 48	$10.00	$ 10	—	$ 2	—	$ 4	—	$ 4	—	$ 4	—	—
Territory 10	2	4.56	146	3.40	34	6.80	54	4.00	20	—	4	—	4	$3.00	6	—	4	—	$ 10
Territory 11	8	2.69	86	1.80	18	9.30	36	—	8	1.00	2	—	6	—	4	—	6	—	4
Territory 12	1	5.10	102	3.30	20	12.50	50	—	4	—	2	—	4	—	4	—	6	—	2
Territory 13	4	3.78	136	3.00	36	8.70	52	7.00	14	3.00	6								
Total		$3.71	$ 564	$2.70	$ 128	$ 8.00	$ 240	$ 9.30	$ 56	—	$ 16	—	$ 18	$10.00	$ 20	—	$ 24	—	$ 18
Western Region																			
Territory 14	10	$2.52	$ 524	$2.40	$ 146	$ 7.40	$ 118	$ 1.90	$ 68	$1.70	$ 24	$1.90	$ 30	$ 1.40	$ 20	$ 8.00	$ 32	$ 5.70	$ 34
Territory 15	16	1.57	380	1.20	122	5.70	102	.60	64	.50	14	.60	14	.70	16	—	10	5.00	20
Territory 16	3	4.21	236	4.20	68	11.50	46	1.60	26	3.00	12	6.00	12	—	10	—	14	6.00	12
Total		$2.28	$1,140	$1.90	$ 336	$ 7.00	$ 266	$ 1.40	$158	$1.10	$ 50	$1.30	$ 56	$ 1.20	$ 46	$ 9.30	$ 56	$ 7.50	$ 66
Total regions		$2.61	$6,272	$2.42	$2,458	$ 5.92	$1,398	$ 1.60	$792	$1.50	$288	$1.50	$248	$ 1.70	$264	$ 7.40	$252	$ 7.50	$256
Government		$6.07	$ 328	$5.60	$ 100	$ 6.50	$ 88	$ 1.10	$ 20	$7.00	$ 14	$4.50	$ 18	$12.00	$ 24	$11.00	$ 22	$ 6.00	$ 12
Total consumer		$2.75	$6,602	$2.53	$2,558	$ 6.30	$1,-86	$ 1.65	$312	$1.57	$302	$1.58	$266	$ 1.76	$288	$ 7.21	$274	$ 7.44	$268

	Total Cookie Product Line	Oatmeal	Butterscotch	Marshmallow	Vanilla	Peanut Butter	Cocoanut	Chocolate	Nut
Variety adv. and s. prom.	$2,402	$1012	$236	$492	$192	$168	$164	$38	$36
Line adv. and s. prom.	$ 46								
Total adv. and s. prom.	$2,868								

*Note: Negative figure = advertising and/or sales promotion $ without G.S.P.C.: computed by dividing advertising and sales promotion $ by −1.

Exhibit 106

though they account for a minimal amount of sales, the fact that they receive almost no marketing effort may cause a distorted or very high profit opportunity rate. Therefore, it is important to portray total dollars with the opportunity rate, so that an indication of the magnitude of the decision and the size of the market is available. The report must show whether the additional profit potential of a product can support an application of additional marketing effort, at the smallest unit of advertising or promotion purchasable within a market. For this reason, the profit opportunity rate and the total profits are both displayed on the statement.

The variety profitability by sales region report provides product management with the means of identifying those areas in which profits or profit opportunity rates differ from expectations. Equipped with this information, product management can work on marketing strategy at the variety level and in specific markets. The tentative nature of decisions at this point must be stressed. The profit opportunity rate summary is intended as a first step. It draws attention to low and high cost, and low and high opportunity areas, without identifying the causes. Once these areas are recognized, it becomes necessary to determine which variables affected profit performance.

Financial and marketing information summary—product line cookies by sales territory. This analysis is shown in Exhibits 107–110 and indicates the following:

- The total gross standard profit contribution earned by the cookie line in each region and territory, and the marketing funds which produced it.
- The extent to which the market "carried" or "was carried by" other markets. This is done by comparison of gross standard profit contribution to the percentage of advertising and sales promotion dollars.
- The profit opportunity rate. This is portrayed for this period and compared with the last period.
- The incremental gross standard profit contribution for a quarter compared with the previous quarter; also, incremental figures are shown for advertising and promotion expenses, products' earnings, and profit opportunity rate.

These figures are shown "netted out." Only the incremental difference or net change is shown.

- The total market size.
- Other available marketing information that may have a bearing upon the earnings of each region and territory, for example, the competitive advertising index and the customer coverage index.

By analyzing these data in terms of trend and performance according to plan and comparing area results against their products' national averages, product management can refine the decisions reached on the basis of the product variety profitability by market summary (see Exhibit 106).

MARKETING/FINANCIAL GUIDELINES

With the aid of marketing/financial guidelines, marketing management can better evaluate alternatives such as "selling off" a regional edition of a magazine, making an addition to a network lineup, adding a product in a line, or adding another line to the company. With these reports, the costs of a specific decision can be more directly related to profits. The primary advantage of this reporting system for product management is that it relates marketing decisions directly to profit rather than to unit movement. More important, this added dimension allows a better identification of profit opportunities, such as:

- Identifying profit opportunities existing in low-franchise areas which would respond to limited tactical increase of marketing funds. Some secondary markets are neglected to such an extent that profits are highly responsive to additional marketing effort. The incremental profits approach allows product managers to measure more adequately the effect of different levels of spending in such areas.
- Identifying areas of relatively higher potential or higher opportunity for products. Special ethnic or demographic cuts can be identified and catered to as high profit opportunity areas.

FINANCIAL AND MARKETING INFORMATION SUMMARY
COOKIE PRODUCT LINE, BY SALES TERRITORY
The National Cookie Company

Eastern Region	Total	Territory 1	Territory 2	Territory 3	Territory 4
Gross standard profit contribution	$ 3,290	$ 698	$1,368	$ 544	$ 580
Advertising and sales promotion	1,184	220	538	210	216
Loss on returns	56	14	14	20	8
Earnings	$ 2,050	$ 464	$ 816	$ 414	$ 356
% G.S.P.C.; % adv. and sales prom.	49.8–49.3	10.5–9.1	20.7–22.2	9.8–8.7	8.8–8.9
Analysis					
Opportunity rate (this qtr.–last qtr.)	2.75–2.90	3.17–2.60	2.54–3.10	3.07–2.20	2.69–3.10
Incremental (this qtr. vs. last qtr.)					
G.S.P.C.	13	33	28	(7)	(41)
A.&P.	105	8	91	5	2
Earnings	(92)	25	(63)	(12)	(42)
Opportunity rate	.12	4.13	.31	—	—
Total market (this qtr. vs. last qtr.)	$11,953	$2,124–1,963	$4,943	$2,415	$2,471
% share of market (this qtr.–last qtr.)	54.5–55.1	64.7–65.5	54.8–59.1	53.1–52.6	46.6–48.4
% distribution		99.0–98.9			
Competitive advertising index		1.40–1.30			
Customer coverage index		95–81			
Shelf space index		1.32–1.01			
Consumption Index—The National Cookie Company		235			
—Competitor A		157			

Exhibit 107

FINANCIAL AND MARKETING INFORMATION SUMMARY
COOKIE PRODUCT LINE, BY SALES TERRITORY
The National Cookie Company

Central Region	Total	Territory 5	Territory 6	Territory 7	Territory 8
Gross standard profit contribution	$ 1,230	$ 448	$ 466	$ 178	$ 188
Advertising and sales promotion	566	194	200	80	92
Loss on returns	44	14	6	10	14
Earnings	$ 670	$ 240	$ 260	$ 88	$ 82
% G.S.P.C.; % adv. and sales prom.	19.4–23.0	6.8–8.0	7.1–8.3	2.7–3.3	2.8–3.8
Analysis					
Opportunity rate (this qtr.–last qtr.)	2.26–2.00	2.31–1.80	2.33–1.90	2.23–3.10	2.04–2.40
Incremental (this qtr. vs. last qtr.)					
G.S.P.C.	(84)	24	(49)	(51)	(8)
A.&P.	(44)	(14)	(29)	(5)	4
Earnings	(40)	38	(20)	(46)	(12)
Opportunity rate	(1.51)	—	(1.69)	(10.20)	—
Total market (this qtr. vs. last qtr.)	$ 6,171	$3,445	$2,328	$760–855	$ 638
% share of market (this qtr.–last qtr.)	41.1–4..3	36.4–35.9	39.9–40.8	46.5–45.6	57.4–52.3
% distribution				98.9–98.9	
Competitive advertising index				2.67–1.95	
Customer coverage index				101–100	
Shelf space index				1.00–.94	
Consumption index—The National Cookie Company				63	
—Competitor A				69	

Exhibit 108

FINANCIAL AND MARKETING INFORMATION SUMMARY
COOKIE PRODUCT LINE, BY SALES TERRITORY
The National Cookie Company

Southern Region	Total	Territory 9	Territory 10	Territory 11	Territory 12	Territory 13
Gross standard profit contribution	$ 564	$ 94	$146	$ 86	$102	$136
Advertising and sales promotion	152	32	32	32	20	36
Loss on returns	64	8	10	18	20	8
Earnings	$ 348	$ 54	$104	$ 36	$ 62	$ 92
% G.S.P.C.; % adv. and sales prom.	8.5–5.5	1.4–1.2	2.2–1.2	1.3–1.1	1.5–.7	2.1–1.3
Analysis						
Opportunity rate (this qtr.–last qtr.)	3.71–3.20	2.94–3.10	4.56–4.44	2.69–1.70	5.10–3.30	3.78–3.80
Incremental (this qtr. vs. last qtr.)						
G.S.P.C.	(3)	(15)	—	4	2	6
A.&P.	(12)	(4)	(3)	(7)	(5)	7
Earnings	9	(11)	3	3	3	(1)
Opportunity rate	(.25)	(3.75)	—	—	—	.86
Total market (this qtr. vs. last qtr.)	$2,185	$ 419	$634–575	$ 353	$299	$480
% share of market (this qtr.–last qtr.)	50.9–49.6	43.7–64.2	45.4–39.2	48.2–48.5	85.5–64.6	57.2–57.8
% distribution			84–83			
Competitive advertising index			1.00–.98			
Customer coverage index			94–93			
Shelf space index			.64–.62			
Consumption index—The National Cookie Company			41			
—Competitor A			46			

Exhibit 109

FINANCIAL AND MARKETING INFORMATION SUMMARY

COOKIE PRODUCT LINE, BY SALES TERRITORY

The National Cookie Company

Western Region	Total	Territory 14	Territory 15	Territory 16	Government	National Average
Gross standard profit contribution	$,140	$ 524	$380	$ 236	$328	
Advertising and sales promotion	500	202	242	56	54	
Loss on returns	52	10	12	10		
Earnings	$ 588	$ 312	$126	$ 170	$274	
% G.S.P.C.; % adv. and sales prom.	17.3–20.0	7.9–8.3	5.8–10.0	3.6–2.3	5.0–2.2	
Analysis						
Opportunity rate (this qtr.–last qtr.)	2.23–2.40	2.59–2.10	1.57–2.30	4.21–3.80		2.40–2.61
Incremental (this qtr. vs. last qtr.)						
G.S.P.C.	(166)	(77)	(70)	(19)		(220)
A.&P.	(33)	(58)	33	(8)		1
Earnings	(133)	(19)	(103)	(11)		(221)
Opportunity rate	(5.03)	(1.33)	—	(2.38)		—
Total market (this qtr. vs. last qtr.)	$4,833	$2,172	$1,632–1,373	$1,020		
% share of market (this qtr.–last qtr.)	46.3–47.8	47.6–46.3	46.5–51.4	45.8–45.2		49.0–49.5
% distribution			96.0–95.9			
Competitive advertising index			3.64–3.15			
Customer coverage index			93–98			
Shelf space index			.78–.84			
Consumption index—The National Cookie Company			39			
—Competitor A			—			

Exhibit 110

This system suggests certain changes in the form of financial data provided to marketing management. These changes do not, and cannot, cover the total distance between imperfect and perfect information. The system shown is a tool to assist in the making and monitoring of marketing decisions. The goal of this system is to present the data in their most usable form, to the end that marketing managers, freed of the need to go through numerous sets of data and reports to comprehend past history, can concentrate their talents on those positive, creative aspects of future planning that promise the best profit potential.

About the Author

SANFORD R. SIMON is a Manager, Management Services with Touche, Ross, Bailey & Smart in New York City. His experience includes work on marketing information systems, inventory control systems, mergers and acquisitions, and marketing and distribution cost analysis projects. Mr. Simon has written for the *Marketing Review* of the American Marketing Association, and managed the study "The Economic Characteristics of Department Store Credit" published by the National Retail Merchants Association in January 1969.